FACING THE RED ARMY IN FESTUNG POSEN

FACING THE RED ARMY IN FESTUNG POSEN

FIRST-HAND ACCOUNTS OF GERMAN SOLDIERS ON THE EASTERN FRONT IN 1945

HANS KLAPA
AND
ALFRED KRIEHN

Translated by Agata Wójcik

Pen & Sword
MILITARY

AN IMPRINT OF PEN & SWORD BOOKS LTD.
YORKSHIRE – PHILADELPHIA

First published in Great Britain in 2023 by
Pen & Sword Military
An imprint of
Pen & Sword Books Ltd
Yorkshire – Philadelphia

The Hunted first published by Hilfdgemeinschaft Ehemaliger Posenkampfer in 1995 as *Von Posen in die Wälder: Hinten den freindlischen Linien uberlebt,* and in Polish by Wydawnicto Pomost in 2020 as *Ludzie, na których się poluje.*

ISBN 978 1 39906 175 9

A CIP catalogue record for this book is available from the British Library.

Typeset in Times New Roman 12/16 by
SJmagic DESIGN SERVICES, India.
Printed and bound in the UK by CPI Group (UK) Ltd.

Pen & Sword Books Ltd. incorporates the Imprints of Pen & Sword Archaeology, Atlas, Aviation, Battleground, Discovery, Family History, History, Maritime, Military, Naval, Politics, Railways, Select, Transport, True Crime, Fiction, Frontline Books, Leo Cooper, Praetorian Press, Seaforth Publishing, Wharncliffe, White Owl and After the Battle.

For a complete list of Pen & Sword titles please contact
PEN & SWORD BOOKS LIMITED
George House, Units 12 & 13, Beevor Street, Off Pontefract Road,
Barnsley, South Yorkshire, S71 1HN, England
E-mail: enquiries@pen-and-sword.co.uk
Website: www.pen-and-sword.co.uk
or
PEN AND SWORD BOOKS
1950 Lawrence Rd, Havertown, PA 19083, USA
E-mail: uspen-and-sword@casematepublishers.com
Website: www.penandswordbooks.com

Contents

Note from the UK Publisher

This volume is compiled of two memoires. Those of Hans Klapa were originally published in German in 1995, and in Polish in 2020. Alfred Kriehn's story has not been published before. The text used in this volume is taken from the Polish translation in both instances.

All original names and spellings have been maintained, but the reader should note that a mixture of Polish and German names for locations and ranks are used throughout. Where possible, the more modern (Polish) names for locations have been used in order to be more familiar to readers. All footnotes have been preserved from the original editions.

The Hunted

Hans Klapa

I dedicate my notes about our joint struggle to my friend and comrade-in-arms, Waldemar Strunk

Note from the Polish Publisher

Hans Klapa's memoires were first published in Dusseldorf in 1995 under the original title *Von Posen in die Wälder: Hinten den freindlischen Linien uberlebt* (From Poznań to the Forest: Surviving behind Enemy Lines), by the German association that helps former soldiers who had fought in Poznań (Hilfsgemeinschaft Ehemaliger Posenkämpfer), edited by Wilhelm Berlemann and Günter Baumann.

All footnotes, unless otherwise stated, have been made by the Polish editors.

The author's original spelling has been preserved, including the inaccurate, and even contemptuous, name for the Russians, 'Ivan', when referring to Red Army soldiers. In order to show how many German veterans viewed the situation shortly after the war, the text has not been censored or corrected in any way by the Polish editors. The author's views expressed in some sections of the text, which could be controversial for Polish (and other) readers, have been commented on by the Polish editors. German and Soviet military ranks are given in their original wording to avoid any doubt when using equivalent ranks from other countries.

Note from the German Editor

This account was written in 1946 and its author has left nothing out. Hans Klappa told about his experiences, his ruthless struggle against the unfavourable forces of both nature and the enemy, whose cruelty was beyond human imagination.[1] Sometimes it is pierced by the shock of military defeat and the sacrifices demanded by war. If pathos resounds here and there, we have not omitted it in order to better favour this drama of German soldiers. After all, their only concern was to defend their Fatherland against a formidable enemy.[2]

Preface by the Author

In reporting the following events, I avoid taking sides. I only want to present the heroic struggle, which, thanks to the highest dedication and commitment, was successful.[3] Participants in the struggle were given the courage and enthusiasm to fight by the memorable words of Marie von Ebner-Eschenbach: 'If there be a faith that can move mountains, it is faith in one's own power.'[4]

Military School

In the first part of my account, I would like to quote the memorable words that adorned the auditorium at our school:[5] 'We erect the portico of the winners of the Third Reich, in marble wrought into a stone dream. When we cannot hold the hammer, build us into the altar's shadow.'

Grey, heavy rain clouds floated across the sky as we left our reserve unit for military school on 8 November 1944. Though we could not erase the horrors of war from our memory, with faces beaming with new hope we sat together – five of us, the inseparable Germans from the West – in the compartment of an eastbound train. As it rolled up to the platform with a thunderous roar, we were welcomed by the towers of Festung Posen [Fortress Poznań], the symbols of this great German city.[6] Our faces clouded over when we received the order to proceed to the training ground. In silence, we boarded the next train, which would take us that evening to the camp and training ground at Warthelager [Biedrusko],[7] 12 kilometres west of Poznań.

It was 20.00. It was very dark outside and heavy rain was falling. We unloaded our heavy suitcases at the destination station,[8] where we were greeted by the military school instructors. Our luggage was loaded onto carts and, freezing, we marched along the muddy streets and roads towards the school, knowing only that we were going to have a hard time. Despite this, we still wondered to ourselves whether we would be happy there. We spent the night on the floor in one of the classrooms. Covered with blankets, we lay down wherever we could.

The next morning it was snowing. As we were waiting for our assignment, we were divided into appropriate units according to our levels of education. The five of us managed to stay together in one class, which we took as a good omen. Classroom 11, to which we were allocated, seemed to be empty. Newly minted NCOs, who had held their farewell party there, had left us their empty bottles as souvenirs. On a plaque on the wall were the words written in capital letters: 'We wish the 3rd Division (III Abteilung) good luck and success!'

By the evening, we had managed to rearrange the classroom and put our things in the lockers. We were about to begin. A teacher's assistant with the rank of Oberfähnrich [chief warrant officer] entered and tried to prepare us for the difficult training ahead. What bothered us most, however, was the lack of food and shortage of fuel for heating. Anyone who had been in such a building before, especially in this region of Germany – rightly called the 'cold homeland' – knew how hard it was to keep warm.

A welcome roll call was planned by the inspection commander for the next day.[9] Long before it, we waited in the dining room of our branch. We, the 180 members of the so-called First Inspection, waited for our commander. Tension was etched on all our faces; this was to be the first meeting with our superior officer who would later decide our fate. And then, he stood before us; our unforgettable Major Hahn.[10] His appearance, posture, voice and simple, true German nature immediately told us that we were dealing with a commander of whom we could be proud. In precise, simple words he explained our study plan and the school's guidelines. We understood every single word.

After the roll call, it soon became clear to us that only the best and most select commanders worked there as training officers. However, what was even more clear was that our time there would be anything but easy. Next, we met our unit commander and had a briefing by our superior officer, who would accompany us throughout our training.

We, the thirty-nine soldiers of the Third Division, which bore the name 'Otto the Great', sat in the large assembly hall, together with the Oberfanrich, in suspenseful anticipation. Over the previous six years our leaders in both study and combat had constantly changed, and now we were waiting for a new one once again. As infantry cadets, we were constantly submitted to fitness tests, both on the battlefield as well as in the garrison. We spared nothing and were able to learn a great deal as a result. We had already passed several exams, but the hardest was yet to come.

Next up came Oberleutnant Heinemann.[11] He was a brave, energetic, handsome officer, who looked at us severely, pursing his lips. He greeted us in a stern but sincere Westphalian manner. The gestures he used to emphasize each of his sentences were strong and accurate. All this allowed us to establish a bond of understanding and trust between us in a short period of time. I was always very pleased to meet a fellow countryman on the Front, and now that our new commander turned out to be a native Westphalian from Detmold, all five of us were filled with pride.

What was next? What was next? The following day, our first timetable was pinned to the notice board. We looked at each other. Training was from 06.00 to 20.00, after which we would study regulations and other additional topics. We started with gymnastic exercises, which were as important a part of training as our intellectual progress. We were subjected to fitness tests, especially in terms of physical endurance.

It rained all morning. The stadium we marched towards looked like a muddy lake. Thank goodness there were only a few slippery spots on the track that surrounded that awful place. With no preparation or proper training, we started a 4,000-metre race straight away. Imagine that: we had barely breathed a sigh of relief after the torments on the Eastern Front and now were stood on the start line in full uniform, except for a hat and a belt. We were tempted to make a joke of it all, but the points we earned in our overall assessment counted towards any future promotion, which forced us to maintain seriousness.

We ran. You had to be able to deploy your forces skilfully if you wanted to survive those ten laps around the stadium. By the sixth lap, I felt my muscles go limp and I was almost disqualified.

But my personal honour and the will to keep going did not allow me to give up and so gave me strength. The last two laps did not resemble a run, rather a mechanical, heavy gait, much like a machine. About 75 per cent of runners reached the finish line this way. Even so, considering the circumstances, I finished in a fairly decent time.

This was followed by grenade throwing and a 100-metre dash, after which the physical examination was over. We gathered in a large assembly hall in the officer's house and listened to a lecture on the Celts by the military school commander. During those first days, our muscles were sore as the result of what our bodies were being put through. We soon resigned ourselves to the fact that all our time to come would be a succession of endurance tests, not to mention the academic results that were obviously expected of us. Nevertheless, we soon we got used to fast pace. Our Oberfeldwebel and Stabsfeldwebel, both of whom were graduates of the school, also failed several times. Whereas we, the younger ones, endured all the hardships of such difficult training with a smile.

Monday usually began with field exercises. We woke up at 05.00 and at 06.00 we had an hour-long tactical lesson. At 07.00 the guns were pulled out and the horses saddled. It is hard to say how much effort it all took, and I often feel that success in such difficult circumstances depends on luck.

The Junker[12] on duty had the most work to do. He was responsible for everything, meaning he had to be able to handle stressful situations and be physically fit to cope with whatever was thrown at him. He was responsible for the general, efficient running of the day, making sure that all the necessary training equipment, including whatever blank ammunition was needed, was at hand. He also needed to ensure that the shooting area where live ammunition was used was fenced off and secured. Throughout the day he needed to lead the unit and report to every superior officer. In addition to these duties, he also received certain privileges that came with being a unit commander. I knew of several times when members of our unit could not sleep at night after being told they would be on duty the next day. Indeed, instead of sleeping and resting, they would study the rules and regulations and make plans for the next day.

As I mentioned before, on Monday mornings the unit would march with the artillery to a huge square, where the soldiers would practise the so-called 'positioning', 'repositioning', 'aiming', etc. It required particular stamina to pull the heavy and light guns together through the deep sand when ordered to 'reposition'. In the meantime, we had a hard time and did our best when trying to aim the weapons, both at the observation point and the firing post.

At noon, we marched. The length of the route was usually 7 to 12 km. After leaving the camp, we would cover the route according to the defined rules. In the camp itself, the entire unit displayed exemplary discipline. It was very important to show respect to any officer you met by making sure everyone marched in parade step. We always enjoyed moments when we marched like this, with our helmets fastened under our chins and making sure we put all our effort into maintaining the correct posture. The clatter of boots on the wide, concrete surfaces of the parade ground sounded like the most beautiful music to us.

After a rather modest dinner, it was then time for supper. Instead of anything to eat, we were given another 'large dose' of discipline, along with a cup of soup or coffee. Breakfast the next morning would consist of a thin, watery, milk-like soup, although compared to the previous day's meal, it tasted very bitter. But we already knew about all this before.

In the afternoon, regardless of the weather, we would have a drill, practise various sports, or study.

Whole afternoons or even whole days were filled with classes. We would alternate between learning combat tactics, the art of command, history lectures, politics, veterinary classes, and even cooking. In the evenings we would die of exhaustion, and then do our homework. But firstly, which was an absolute necessity, the support staff went out to search for wood. Many funny situations would occur at this time and on one evening, our comrade, Waldemar, tried to arrest an armed Polish policeman who was guarding a timber yard.[13]

We would collect various elements of wooden fences and posts to keep our room warm. One of the funniest moments was when our comrade from Mulheim took someone to help him and returned with a birch trunk 20 cm in diameter and 4-5 m long. A fallen tree that lay beside two others on a remote incline, which we had always used as our basic landmark during target and shooting practice, had now been cut down and served to us all. We laughed at this for a long time.

In the evenings we usually had a 'memory hour', where we would show each other photographs, read and write letters and think about our homes. Then we got down to work. Everything was very well organized. Each of us worked on something different and how the concept of 'collective work' had developed in our country over time. Otherwise, some of our comrades would just sit until morning, either writing or studying.

On Thursday mornings, we would shoot with live ammunition. All weapons were used in a premediated order. The commander always awarded prizes for good results, which usually consisted of white bread or other delicacies. We always made sure every effort was made. We were motivated by our commander's memorable words that nobody would become a Leutnant [lieutenant] in his inspection unless they learned to shoot properly. After the afternoon training, a four-hour night exercise was carried out.

Saturdays and Sundays were slightly different from the other days of the week. If we had any free time, we would go to the camp cinema. On Sunday, those who were more daring would go to Poznań, if they were

FACING THE RED ARMY IN FESTUNG POSEN

lucky. The main charm of the city was the food. Heinz from Berlin had particular skills in this area and could eat five or six dishes one after the other. Apart from that, Sunday afternoons were quiet and we would use the time to prepare ourselves for the coming week. It would not be fair to talk about having free time during such a busy training course. We constantly had to learn and be active if we wanted to achieve our goals.

When it came to discipline and order in the school, I can say with confidence that everything was very well organized. The garrison I was in housed 100,000 soldiers.[14] In such cases, the discipline and order required in these educational institutions were usually of an exceptional nature. Despite this, someone was still punished every day. One of our commanders was a real 'firebrand' when it came to following the rules. Every offence was punished severely and hard, with the most common penalty being imprisonment. But an even worse penalty was that the person being punished also had to write a 10-20-page essay on some complicated topic. One day, two comrades left the bathhouse five minutes early and were sentenced to three days of severe detention and had to write an essay on 'political Catholicism according to *The Myth of the Twentieth Century*'.[15] I rarely saw people punished as severely as those two soldiers. They looked completely devastated. A cadet from a neighbouring unit once said that it was just as hard to survive in our company without being punished as it was to complete our studies successfully. It was a fair point. Over time, we also underwent training in the field of law and would learn the whole range of penalties available for even the smallest of offences.

Classes with the commander had their own special character. You not only had to listen carefully to his lectures and make notes about the most important issues, but also had to think logically in order to be able to answer his questions. During his classes, you could see the Junkers break out in a cold sweat. Classes with our squad leader were also very strict. His specialty was to appoint one of us as commander and then that person had to present a particularly difficult case (which the squad leader would invent) and then explain it. It really was very hard.

Major Eberhard Hahn at one of the post-war meetings of the association that helped veterans who had fought at Poznań. The former commander of the 1st Inspection of the Wehrmacht's 5th Infantry Cadet School in Poznań, he was considered among his subordinates as one of the most strict and ruthless officers.

Particular importance was attached to the art of free, unforced verbal expression. Firstly, you had to give a lecture on a selected topic, and then conduct classes for non-commissioned officers and even classes for the company commander. After the lecture, the conclusions were drawn, but they needed to be very precise and consist of several elements: the lecturer's attitude and posture;

preparation; mastery of the topic; and logical structure. Woe to him who, in the final analysis, was not objective and was guided by kindness or benevolence.

Every now and again we were tested on our general knowledge. This was because such knowledge would be useful later for those destined to become officers. In the meantime, training exercises took place for all units stationed at Warthelager.

After six weeks we had our first social evening for the entire unit. Its aim was to get to know each other outside of work. There was usually some form of celebration at that time of year in a nearby farm, but that year it was abandoned because of the absence of Countess von Treskau and the other ladies in her circle of friends.[16]

It was now approaching Christmas, and that particular Christmas Eve will stay in my memory forever. I do not know what is about this day in that it only becomes important in the evening. Due to a violent storm, we did not report outside the artillery room. Within ten minutes, Oberleutnant Heinemann's gymnastic exercises finished us off to such an extent that we had no idea what was going on. The unfavourable weather made any further training and afternoon classes impossible. In the evening, our unit celebrated Christmas in the lecture hall. The room was festively decorated, and we sat at long tables covered with white tablecloths. Each of us has a plate of sweet treats, but our thoughts naturally turned to our homeland and our loved ones now more than ever. The celebrations took place in a unique, strict, military way. Many of us were surprised that of all the Christmas carols we knew, the only one we heard was 'Hohe Nacht der klaren Sterne'. The radio in the corner was broadcasting Christmas carols and directed our thoughts homeward. I was particularly impressed by the transmission from the fortress at St. Nazaire,[17] where my brother was posted.

Meanwhile, our commander was called to Poznań to receive his promotion to Hauptmann. As soldiers in his unit, we were all very proud of his achievement.

At Christmas, some of us were able to have visitors on both holidays, but we were all allowed a good rest. We decorated a Christmas tree beautifully, and our 'memory hour' by candlelight was a very special experience. Our thoughts were with our homeland and the letters we wrote were full of longing, which can only be understood by those who have spent five or six Christmases away from home.

Over these two festive days, the food tasted wonderful. We beamed at each other as a pound of sausage was placed in our hands and we could finally eat our fill after such a long time. On the day after Christmas, the unit gathered together in the evening for a big celebration, forgetting for a moment about our soldierly duties.

When the holidays were over, we were pleased to see that our Hauptmann had a softer expression on his face. The year 1944 was coming to an end and we spent the last moments of the old year in our room with a bottle of cognac. The eleven of us wished each other joy and hoped that we would soon achieve our training goals.

Early in the morning of 1 January 1945, a new group of cadets joined the roll call. The commander of our school, Oberst Gonell, took the opportunity for us to renew the oath and our sacred obligations. Some of us received promotions; six members of our unit became Wachtmeisters or sergeants, which encouraged us all to work even harder.

In the first days of January, we gathered together in the vast cinema hall to listen to our training commander, Oberleutnant von Olsberg. In emphatic words he presented to us a picture of the truly great tradition of the German officer corps. Of particular note was when he spoke of his pride in his noble title, which was awarded (along with the rank of officer) to his grandfather for his special achievements in years gone by.

The next day was another study day. Early in the morning we went out into the field to train, march and learn many new things. It all gave us great joy and every time we started to lose strength, we would hear the words, 'It's not over yet!' So, we gritted our teeth and continued on.

Grand Manoeuvres

The troops stationed in Warthelager and Poznań were tasked with demonstrating their readiness and strike capabilities through extensive combat exercises. The elite of this project were the Fahnenjunkers from the 5th Cadet School. Artillery, anti-aircraft, Luftwaffe and assault gun units in Poznań also took part in these manoeuvres.[18]

The positions of individual units were as follows: Festung Posen was defended by inspections from the 5th Infantry Cadet School,[19] fortress units and all types of troops stationed in the city. The role of attackers

Assault gun from the 500th Assault Gun Training and Reserve Squadron during the ceremony in the barracks at Golęcin. This unit, along with other 'Poznań' units, took part at the end of January 1945 in the German troop manoeuvres that simulated the assault and defence of Poznań.

was to be played by the so-called 'IV Siberian Corps'[20] formed of Fahnenjunkers from the training group at Warthelager and other units stationed there. The attack was to come from the east, from Swarzędz [Schwersenz] and to move parallel to the runway.[21] Its aim was to break through the outer fortification system as quickly as possible, make a thorough reconnaissance of the area, and finally capture the city.

The manoeuvres were set to being on 13 January 1945 at 06.00 sharp. By that time, the concentration area (forest areas within a radius of approximately 3 km to the east of the fortification system) had to be manned. When all the positions in Warthelager were set, the march to the launching area began around noon. We had about 13 km to cover and reached the designated part of the forest in the evening. Due to the prevailing cold and huge amounts of snow that still covered the fields, we received special permission to light small fires. We had no appropriate winter clothing and did not want to catch frostbite.

Together with two other comrades, we were assigned to a light artillery unit as reinforcement for the company and were under strict orders. We wandered around the woods for some time before coming across a group of cadets who were warming themselves by a small fire, so we spent the cold night hours talking together in conversation.

Early in the morning, at 06.00, we heard the signal that signified the start of the manoeuvres. First, reconnaissance units were sent towards the enemy, while in the meantime, heavy weapons were deployed in firing positions. The well-established telephone network and proven radio links were used to ensure success. After a massive artillery attack involving all kinds of heavy weaponry, an attack was launched on the fortress under the cover of tanks. The fighting troops were accompanied by observers, while additional equipment and shortages in the numbers of units and armaments made the whole thing seem very real.

The sun broke through the clouds and illuminated the impressive sight in all its magnificence. We looked down at the approaching armoured vehicles from above. After the heavy artillery and assault guns had attacked, the operation continued. Once again, it turned out that well-armed fortifications, built in the 1870s[22] and used during the Great War, were not insurmountable obstacles.

A staff composed of ten generals and a large number of commanders observed the course of the manoeuvres from the famous Fort Kernwerk.[23] The propaganda company and various people from film and radio companies watched the action and recorded what was happening in words and images.[24] In addition, Himmler and Guderian from the Reich General Staff came to see the courage of the fighting units for themselves.[25]

The attack was going well and Luftwaffe units were also soon involved in the exercise. Despite staunch defence, the attackers could not be prevented from breaking into the city. More and more areas gave up resistance and at about noon, the attackers were already stood on the banks of the Warta. The eastern part of the city was now in our hands. Then the command to 'stand down' was sounded.

The mission had been a success. Moreover, we had achieved an additional success, as the soldiers of the IV Siberian Corps had emerged victorious. Only one of us guessed that eight days later, the real Russian corp would reach Poznań along the same road we had trodden, and we ourselves would be the heroic defenders of the fortress. Perhaps our laughter and joy on that bright winter day was silenced too quickly.

Black Clouds on the Eastern Front

I remember those happy days when we advanced quickly towards Ternopil [in Ukraine]. I was now sad to see that the Russians were doing the same in the opposite direction. We learned from the daily newspapers and radio coverage that they were preparing an offensive on two fronts with about 100 divisions. The latest reports gave us a lot of detailed information.

On 18 January 1945, we heard the latest news during a training exercise. The enemy had managed to achieve significant gains in a couple of places, as the battle for Warsaw continued. We learned about the operations near Toruń and thought about the cadets from the infantry school there.[26] In those hard days, our commander would tell us to speak to the soldiers in our companies to increase morale. Even in a hopeless situation, we had to be able to motivate them and lift their spirits. It was not easy. Later, the matter of the Volksturm, which was very topical at the time, was brought up, which showed how serious the situation was.

About noon, we had time to read *Mein Kampf*. Each word was filled with great power: 'Even after thousands of years, no one will talk about heroism without thinking of the German Army during the world war. From the mists of the past, the grey steel of helmets will emerge as a monument to immortality. As long as Germany lives, the knowledge that these people were sons of this nation will continue.'

In the evening, I took the opportunity to phone my fiancée, but our connection was constantly interrupted by anti-aircraft alerts. The enemy gave us no respite. Our homeland was under constant attack. I told her about the hardships we experienced at school, coupled with

After the offensive launched on 12-14 January from the Vistula River, meeting only slight enemy resistance, troops of Marshal Zhukov's 1st Belorussian Front were rapidly approaching Poznań. This image shows Red Army soldiers heading west in the winter of 1945.

our eagerness to achieve our goals. When she asked when I would get leave, I told her that it would probably in March or April, 'if Ivan allowed'. I used those words not because I had a feeling of what was about to happen, but because something came over me. That was probably the last long-distance call I had to my homeland.

At roll call the next day, we received information about the lifting of the curfew that was introduced during our earlier manoeuvres. At the same time, a state of full mobilization was declared. From now on, we were not allowed to leave the barracks. Our unit became an infantry unit, more precisely, an infantry platoon. Apart from three of our comrades, the rest of us were to stay together in room 11. And so, in the evening, Peter from Gelsenkirchen, Günter from Witten and Helmut from Iserlohn packed their things and went off to become battalion liaison officers. Waldemar and I tried to give them the proper equipment. We worked frantically. Preparation and organization were very important, especially in all the rush. Meanwhile, our hour of departure was approaching.

The March to Poznań

It was time to bid farewell to the camp in Warthelager. A chapter of our life was coming to an end, full of hardships as well as successes, although we all had imagined that moment differently. We were overwhelmed by the shadow of the approaching front.

With sadness, we packed our backpacks, taking with us all the memories from the last weeks. We took our luggage to the lecture hall, from where it would be taken to the railway station. Our training officers' suitcases were also there, giving us a sense of certainty as to their destination.

There was a lot to do in the office. The final documents were packed up. We brought our map cases, which we had used during manoeuvres, and were given provisions for the road. Once again, each of us checked our weapons and equipment. Waldemar and I were part of the telephone unit, and when the time came, we would later show our skills in the East. We heard the shouts of command and gathered in line, before beginning the march towards Poznań. Our commander, on horseback, turned back towards us and greeted us with shouts of encouragement. Our military tactics teacher was stood at the crossroads. 'Just don't forget the basic tactical concepts!' he shouted to us, smiling. Soon we had left the Warthelager barracks behind us. We had a short break, during which time the latest mail was distributed. We did not know at the time that these were the last letters we would receive, but we greedily absorbed the news from our loved ones, as if we sensed the importance of the moment.

Sitting on a stone roadside post, I read letters from my parents and fiancée, line by line. I remembered a fragment from our last telephone conversation: 'Only if Ivan doesn't do anything bad again.' I had a feeling that today those words would come true. Perhaps people at home already sensed that the fate of Germany would be decided here, near Poznań? However, my thoughts were interrupted by the order to continue marching.

It started to snow. We reached the outskirts of Poznań late in the afternoon and could see the defensive preparations around the city's fortifications, especially the camouflage measures. Here and there, 88-mm anti-aircraft guns were being put into position, their lowered barrels suggesting that we could expect enemy tanks. The civilians in Poznań were showing signs that they were nervous; even on the faces of the Poles one could see the fear of what awaited us all.

We marched through the suburbs, passing vast parks full of trees, and huge villas with gardens. All this, together with the wide streets we walked down, left us in no doubt that Poznań was a great German city. People waved at us. We entered the yard of the 'Kleist' barracks.[27] We were given rooms and food, then our first orders arrived. In the evening, Waldemar talked about taking part in various special actions and the possibilities of promotion. We wrote messages to our loved ones and dropped the letters into the mailbox by the gate with mixed feelings. Would they reach their destinations?

Meanwhile, it was officially announced that the majority of our unit was to be disbanded.[28] The radio operators were transferred to special units with the commanders. I myself did not know anything about my fate yet. In the meantime, Waldemar was fighting with his superiors for us to stay together in the company. Due to recent events, he managed to keep me with him. Thanks to you, Waldemar, only today do I recognize the seriousness of the situation at that time. Thanks also to you, Providence, who in that hour decided both of our fates: 'If you have a good companion, you can go with him to the end.'

This was the beginning of our common struggle of perseverance. It gradually became clear which members of our Third Division had completed their training the best, and we could see the decision of who to assign to certain units was fair. I would have loved to call home once more, but nobody was allowed to leave the barracks. Early the next morning, our infantry division took up their firing positions. At the eastern end of the barracks, we set up our observation post in a small hall. Next to it, on the left flank, was a bunker with anti-aircraft ammunition for the artillery. A frosty, foggy, winter day was dawning, and we strained our eyes to try to see through the mist. We were all on full alert. I learned from the artillery officer that the outer fortifications were armed with 1,500 88-mm anti-aircraft guns.[29] We would give the Russians a warm welcome.

In the evening, we received an order to change positions, so we dismantled our observation point to prepare for a new operation.

Waiting for the Enemy

We now prepared to take up our positions in the outer fortifications at the eastern end of the city. Marching through streets for the last time, we enjoyed the unforgettable impression that this truly German city offered. As we passed through the vast square, we admired the Imperial Castle. Then we passed the city's theatre and administration buildings. The sun was shining, making the castle, the symbol of the city, shine brightly. We had fallen in love with these places during our training and now we realized that we would defend them to the last drop of our blood.

Meanwhile, the citizens, showing their liveliness, bustled about in a hurry. We were met by columns of refugees fleeing towns further east. You could see the pain of what it meant to lose one's homeland etched on the faces of these people, who had never before felt the horrors of war so closely.

We crossed a large bridge over the River Warta and turned left, towards the forts. Along this entire section, along embankments and bunkers up to Fort IV 'Hake' and Fort IIIa 'Prittvitz', we could see armoured vehicles preparing for combat operations. Artillery units had already taken up their positions and were firing practice shots.

After receiving coordinates from our commander, myself and my colleagues in the communications unit went with the NCO to the observation post to work out what communications network would need to be established. Half an hour later, a telephone connection was set up between the observation post and the firing post. The guns were in position and so in the afternoon, we started firing towards key targets on the horizon. It would now remain to be seen whether our shooting skills acquired at training school would prove themselves in combat.

Preliminary preparations were completed by the evening and so we headed to the observation post. We dug under a 1-metre thick, heavy concrete object, making ourselves a bombproof and anti-shrapnel bunker. A few traces on the concrete revealed to us that it must have been a machine gun post during the last war, and we even used the trench system that had been left over from before, although unfortunately, it was impossible to make them any deeper because the ground was frozen.

We now had an opportunity to look around at what was in front of us. Below was a large factory building, which served as a warehouse for food and other industrial goods manufactured for the Waffen-SS. It appeared that the depository was slow to distribute its resources, so we brought each other as much sausage and wine as we could carry in our hands. We also took a few cases of French cognac to provide essential protection against the cold nights. The discovery of a few bags of candy drops and caramels brought particular joy, and we were now very well stocked for the upcoming nights.

The next morning, we fired a barrage at the space between us and the enemy, while rolling stock units replenished the ammunition bunker. Our platoon headquarters, consisting of four light infantry guns, was quite unfortunate. The whole unit (apart from camp) lived in a very beautiful manor house near the firing post, and it was really sad to see those good carpets and floors suffer under the weight of the soldiers' heavy boots. Meanwhile, the other units went out to bring winter and camouflage clothing from the warehouses. By the early evening, our entire unit was fully kitted out with equipment, which in terms of value and quantity was quite amazing.

Tremendous amounts of food had been collected and we had the best things at our disposal. There was no shortage of tobacco products or alcoholic beverages anywhere, meaning the mood in the units was rather special. The mere presence of 1,200 students from the 5th Cadet School inside the fortifications of Poznań was perhaps the best guarantee that the combat units would pass the most difficult of practical exams.

The next day, along with the rest of the heavy artillery, firing exercises were carried out, thus demonstrating the firepower of this east-facing part of the fortress. Waldemar and I took turns at the observation post every half day, quickly writing a few words of greeting to our loved ones in our free time. 'Dear homeland, rest easy! We will manage.' This was probably what the majority of letters from Poznań said. Weapons and equipment, combined with the good morale of the unit, allowed us to grow in the belief that we would be able to handle anything. Let the enemy come.

The Beginning of the Battle

I think the date was 25 January 1945.[30] In the early afternoon, we received a report that a Russian armoured unit of about 400 tanks was heading towards Poznań via a wide road from Swarzędz. One had the impression at times that the Russian units choose the same attack route as our 'IV Siberian Corps' once did. The three of us sat at the observation post and watched the enemy's movements. We were ready. What was curious, however, was that we could not understand his intentions. With time, we learned to accept the fact that our opponent had very long-range plans and, as we found out, he did not intend – as we had previously thought – to take the fortress by storm.

The Russians circumvented Poznań on both sides to enter the city from the west, and we watched as the vast majority of their troops continually moved westward. We slowly realized that we were surrounded. Our time was coming. Fierce fighting was already waging on the western edge of the city. Our 88-mm anti-aircraft batteries were not allowing the tanks to overwhelm our defences.

Bombers and attack airplanes arrived, their hundreds of bombs and missiles carpeting the entire area. Fires were breaking out everywhere and it seemed like the whole city was on fire. The demon of war raged with tremendous fire. We knew that we had to be on our guard, and soon the enemy began its first attack. After a short burst of light artillery and mortars, a battalion-sized unit was heading our way. Unfortunately, I was unlucky enough to be the telephonist at the combat position that afternoon. However, as NCOs, Waldemar Strunk and Hans Metzler kept me up to date about what was happening out there. This meant I could take the opportunity to warn the gun crew. With sadness, I told them about the news from the battlefield, and so soon our battery was firing with great power. The observers informed me of our first successes, which I immediately passed on to the artillerymen. My comrades at the guns smiled, knowing how important it was to get the upper hand. Then another report arrived saying that the rest of the Russian battalion was turning around and retreating like crazy to their starting positions.

We proudly reported to our commander that the enemy's attack on our positions, made with the strength of a battalion, had been stopped by the devastating firepower of our infantry platoon. We were happy with our initial victory, but we were also aware that the enemy would try again. I went to the observation point to replace Waldemar. I could now see for myself that the Russians had left about forty dead on the battlefield.

After a while, our commander appeared. Meanwhile, the enemy was sending attack planes back into action again, which constantly attacked us with bombs and onboard weapons. The news of our promotion to the rank of lieutenant for the special dedication we had shown was received amidst the bangs and whistles of enemy shells. We were happy and proud of achieving this ambitious goal from an excellent military school. We all knew it was not easy. Our communication officers crawled over to be the first to applaud us: 'Herr Leutnant, let me congratulate you!' We heard the sharp sound of the telephone and for the first time, I answered with my new rank. I could feel the importance of the moment. I wanted to see my loved ones and tell them that my dreams had just come true. At company headquarters, we received our new documents and found out that as many as twenty-six soldiers from our unit of thirty-nine had received a promotion. Waldemar could barely contain his joy. When I spoke to him on the phone, he was already answering in a booming voice: 'Reserve Leutnant Strunk here!'

A German telephonist on duty on the Eastern Front.

That evening, our colleagues from the regiment visited us,[31] including Peter Ohs and Günter Hausherr, who came with a special mission: to bring us our new insignia. They had both returned from the tailors in the city and let us try on our fabulous new uniforms (leather coats). They were made from the best quality leather with extra additions. Our once inseparable foursome was together again, and we rejoiced and renewed our friendship with a bottle of wine. Waldemar and I quickly wrote letters to loved ones, which our colleagues said they would send by plane.

Meanwhile, our platoon's headquarters was moved to one of the military artillery shelters. Equipped with heating, running water and beds, this square concrete bunker provided the best possible protection. There was a clothing store in one of the rooms, so now we could wear clean, fresh underwear every day. A soap factory nearby even provided us with the best cleaning products. Of particular interest to us in another room was the huge store of radio transmitters, where the best and most expensive radio transmitters for export were stored. Naturally, each of us appropriated a couple of items. I took a small handheld radio produced by the Super company and an Italian receiver.

The food was so good and plentiful that all day long we paid no attention to our mess tins. We ate biscuits thickly smeared with butter almost constantly, and enjoyed the most excellent wines, including red and white Mosel. Our needs here were certainly taken care of.

The next day, we were all in combat readiness from the early hours of the morning. Once again, we had to repel the Russian attacks. Their mortar shells were coming from everywhere and although our positions were beyond their reach, this did not mean that their attacks were any less persistent and tiring. Moreover, snipers had joined the action and were especially keen on targeting the exit from our bunker. Every time someone tried to come in or out, bullets would whizz over their heads.

We also knew that the enemy was attacking the western side of the city the hardest, and we could hear the endless sound of a continuous cannonade from there. The famous 'Katyushas' [Soviet rocket launchers] fired almost constantly, as thick smoke engulfed the city. Unfortunately, the enemy managed to breach the defences and took the Imperial Castle. The airfield [Zeppelinwiese][32] was under fire from the Russians and as a result, we received our supplies via an air bridge. At night, planes would make parachute drops of containers with weapons and ammunition. Then the next morning, our lead NCO and I would observe the area carefully. After a while, we would recognize every tree and bush. One time, our attention was particularly drawn to two small haystacks, where some Russians were always busy bustling around. We needed to confirm, at all costs, that both haystacks were in fact hiding heavy tanks. Our guns were ready to fire and a couple of minutes later, I give the first command to shoot. After the shells had landed, we saw bits of hay camouflage flying around. The calibre of our guns was not sufficient enough to penetrate the machines' armour, but we considered it a success that the right tank had been immobilized, while the other one moved to hide behind a house.

In the afternoon we saw a tank moving back and forth on the hill in front of us. With the help of some scissor binoculars, I could see its 8-metre barrel and realized it was an IS.[33] At the top of the hill, the machine stopped and turned its turret towards us. Next, it slowly lowered its barrel and aimed right at the centre of our observation post. The hairs on my skin stood up; I felt that this was it for us.

I bent down and looked carefully into the mouth of his barrel through my binoculars. The tank froze and moved further to the left, before starting to fire violently at the nearby ammunition depot. It hit the target with great force, and with every shot large amounts of explosives blasted into the air with a bang. The tank crew were clearly confident that the Russian reconnaissance had established the site was undefended. The anti-tank gun was on the other side of the building.

The cannonade lasted for a good half an hour, directed all the time from the commander in the tank's turret. However, the attack was interrupted by a Panzerfaust shot fired by a young German NCO. The tank hatch flew up into the air and the resulting huge column of fire was probably the most beautiful sight of the day for a young soldier in our unit. Once again, the individual training we had undergone at Warthelager was proving to have been successful.

The first orders of the day were issued and we received radio telegrams from the high command in Berlin. With disgust and indignation, we received the news that the commander of the fortress, who wanted to escape the city by air [Editor's note: a rumour that did not correspond to the facts and was spread by Poles], had been removed. After being promoted to the rank of general, his place was taken by the commander of our 5th Cadet School, Ernst Gonnel. This was certainly a great honour.

Then came the first reports of victories at the front, where over sixty tanks had been destroyed, weapons and ammunition had been seized, and countless enemy soldiers taken prisoner. Most importantly, however, the attack by seven Russian divisions had been steadfastly resisted.

On the last day of January, we had to move our observation post forward slightly to get to one of our infantry companies. It was morning when, together with one of my telephonists, I had to stretch the long telephone cable out to the front without any cover. The enemy was sitting in his position about 300 metres from us and fired furiously with machine guns. But we had to obey our orders and as we unwound the cable along the trench, I tied one end to my waist and carefully crawled forward. A few metres behind me, the telephone operator followed with the equipment. It took some time before the Russians realized that we were right under their noses, but soon their machine guns attacked even more ferociously. We fell down hard into the snow, and I remembered what had been said to us: 'I expect you to rise to the top of your abilities when the going gets tough. You are the defenders of the Millennial Reich, my dear officers. You will be responsible for all of Germany. In those moments you will have to go beyond yourselves and say, "now it is up to us". Wherever you are, you will always have your comrades by your side. You cannot afford weakness. You must always set an example to others.' I turned to my operator and met his sympathetic gaze. Making the decision to crawl further head, I remembered more important words: 'I wish in those desperate hours you could say to the whole German nation, "Look how your officers are fighting!"'

We continued moving slowly, further and further forward, before finally leaping into a bomb crater to hide. After returning, we quickly connected our telephone to the power supply and were soon receiving the first reports from the various observation posts and firing positions. Diagonally to our left, the commander of a light mortar platoon was lying on the ground, and both platoons were now firing to relieve the left company.

On 1 February, there were changes to the composition of our unit. Half of it (ie two cannons), were to be assigned to an adjacent battalion.[34] Waldemar was appointed to company headquarters as a communications commander, to replace another inexperienced officer there. I, on the other hand, was appointed the platoon's communications commander and I took action immediately.

In the evening we built a firing position near the Ostmühle[35] mill, in the village of Główna [Glowno]. We left our guns in the garden of an isolated villa and set up an observation point on the top (fifth) floor of the mill. The observation possibilities from this place were excellent, but we were also aware of the danger in the event of a possible air raid. There were several hundred barrels of wheat in the building, and the mill itself had very modern equipment.

To protect against possible shrapnel, on the company command's advice we filled two sacks of wheat and built a makeshift shelter. We

Ostmühle, the mill at Nadolnik, where the author and his comrades spent many days during the battle for Poznań.

stacked the sacks on top of each other, constructing walls and even a ceiling from them. We then sat together in our wheat bunker with our scissor binoculars, while our artillerymen soon started firing at enemy positions.

Dark February

In the cellar of the Ostmühle was a white-tiled dressing room, which was where we set up our accommodation. We collected furniture from nearby abandoned houses, even putting a thick Persian rug on the floor. Next, we brought a sofa, table and chairs. One of us found a small stove from somewhere, while someone else found a small table with an ashtray and an armchair. We laid down thick mattresses on the floor for sleeping. We were glad to have electricity, which was powered from the cellar by the mill's generator. Thanks to that we had light and, most importantly, we could tune our radios. The company command post was about 500 metres away in the cellar of one of the abandoned houses, and soon all our equipment was working properly. In suspense, we listened to the news about the situation in Poznań's fortress. From this we found out that the right front had already reached the Oder. We were fighting like lions to break the Russian strike force. Bloody street fights were taking place in the city centre. With the strength of its six divisions (about 40,000 men), they were slowly pushing forward. The courage of the defenders was extraordinary, and hand-to-hand combat was common. In addition, the Panzerfausts had turned out to be extremely destructive weapons. They were very effective because they could be used from the high floors of buildings, thus constituting an impenetrable barrier for armoured vehicles from moving into a given street. The number of enemy tanks destroyed in this way had already reached 100.

In one of the forts defending the access to the city centre [Editor's note: 'Old Grolmann' fort], young officers prepared Panzerfausts for action, and the approaching Russians were greeted with heavy fire from these weapons. Meanwhile, the enemy had increased the rate of fire on our part of the city, pulling up the heavy guns and Katyushas to smoke out those of us defending the eastern part of the city. It turned out, however, that we had the same fighting spirit as our colleagues in the city's western part.

Disturbances and breakdowns occurred constantly. Repaired connections were systematically broken. Waldemar often wandered about trying to repair damaged telephone cables, lying for hours under the heaviest fire to find a way through the rubble and debris. On the left bank of the Warta, the enemy was occupying an increasingly bigger area, and we could clearly see him on the other side of the river. The morale of the troops stayed strong, as we still hoped reinforcements would arrive and had faith that we would finally hear the roar of the guns of the approaching relief. Unfortunately, it was a vain hope, because we were fully aware that the main front was already near Kostrzyn.

Waldemar and I took the opportunity to visit our colleagues Peter and Günter. Their regiment's headquarters[36] was located in a cellar near the famous 'Nivea' factory. It was very risky to reach them under the constant bombardment, but they both welcomed us very warmly, as they always did. We had a lot to say to each other, especially about our families, wondering what they would think as they listened to the messages from Poznań. We arranged a return visit to our headquarters in Ostmühle for the following evening.

The mill manager, a Pole, provided us with a sack of fresh bread for the occasion. I prepared three big plates of buttered bread rolls, accompanied by coffee, wine, beer and cognac. Large quantities of tobacco were also available. That evening, we met together down in the cellar. Waldemar welcomed our guests and we sat down in our quarters: Peter, Günter, Waldemar, Heinz Stoll (from Berlin), Hanz Metzler (from Garmisch) and myself. We talked about our dreams with a good cigarette and a glass of wine. Heinz was particularly optimistic, constantly telling us about his plans for the future. We parted ways late in the evening, accompanied, as usual, by heavy Russian bombers (we called them 'Iron Gustavs').

Many people had already died during these bombings, but that night was especially bad. Early in the morning, at 06.00, Waldemar came to us to adjust the transmitter and told us that a shell had hit our headquarters. He said that our friend Heinz had been killed and that he had been pulled out from under the rubble with four other officers. Peter and Günter had fled in terror. I called Peter a little later, and he happily told me about his miraculous survival.

The Russians had been launching massive shell fire from anti-tank guns and tanks towards our positions since the early hours. This meant we constantly had to crawl outside in search of broken telephone lines. I remembered that murderous fire, having seen those guns in action when I fought in Russia. I often fell to the ground and lay motionless for minutes on end, afraid to raise my head. Our position was becoming more and more desperate. Air deliveries were interrupted and we had to be satisfied with the ammunition we had, although we did not know how long it would last.

In the meantime, we heard on the radio that the soldiers from the cadet school at Toruń had broken out from the encirclement after heavy fighting. From now on, we also thought about the same, and even food was provided for the journey. However, the planned breakout did not happen as we were unable to keep our plans secret. Not only Polish civilians, but also our enemies knew about it, so it was finally decided to defend the city to the last soldier. New positions and firing posts were created in the gardens and alleys, with all troops preparing for 'encirclement defence'. We also started to dig trenches and build embankments.

One of our NCOs was our friend from the south, a German with the rank of Unteroffizier. Everyone knew him for his extraordinary courage. At the head of two units, he took part in reconnaissance operations, breaking through the encirclement ring in the east. His successes were widely known, but completely useless after the order to break out of the encirclement was cancelled. He was personally very disappointed about this and drowned his anger in alcohol.

In the evening of 13 February, the order was given to carry out a third reconnaissance, this time to Warthelager, about 12 km from Poznań. The unit was supposed to make some important reconnaissance there. Our colleague, this time dressed in civilian clothes and armed only with a pistol, bid us farewell, sensing that he may never return. The next day, we could no longer remember him. The city was still defended around the Citadel and on the eastern bank of Warta. The enemy bombarded the districts we occupied from all sides, showering us in a hail of missiles. The houses were all in ruins and there was a terrible pounding everywhere.

The Polish civilians were also slowly losing their spirits. The mill manager asked me where the front actually was, so I simply smiled and asked if he was afraid too: 'No,' he said, 'I personally don't care who is here, Germans or Russians!' I said a few words of goodbye and left him.

The enemy had smashed our neighbouring battalion, so we had lost contact with the part of our platoon that was with it. Waldemar tried to establish contact with them. All afternoon he walked back and forth, but our losses were severe. Many of our colleagues had died and the last sparks of optimism in us were fading. We slowly began to prepare for a heroic death. As we dug the trenches, we felt that we were digging our graves. Waldemar spoke to his superior commander, who asked him if he was ready to die. Waldemar did not seem to understand the question. The commander said that he had neither a wife nor children, so parting with this beautiful world could not be too hard for him. When Waldemar told him about his parents, the commander waved his hand. When death approaches, everyone is lost in their own thoughts.

We fought and persevered, but we were no match for the brave Leutnants from Metz.[37] I myself was convinced that we had done our duty. Now, when it came to dying, I was firmly resolved to enter the great afterlife with flags flying. The moment had come when fidelity to an idea must be proved not only on the eve of birth, but also on the eve of death.

Map showing the northern region of Poznań, with Subsection III of the German defence system of Festung Posen marked. Towns north of Poznań, with the training ground at Warthelager [Biedrusko] are also marked.

Breaking the Encirclement

It was late afternoon on 15 February 1945. In the eastern part of Poznań, fierce battles were still taking place, but the confidence of the defenders was slowly weakening. Everyone could feel it in the atmosphere. The latest orders to dig in and fight to the last soldier did not have a positive effect on morale. Each man wondered about his own fate. The fifth floor of the Ostmühle had been destroyed, so we moved our observation point one floor down. From there we could see the other bank of the Warta and observe how the Russians were gradually taking over the area. I watched in horror as large groups of German soldiers ran around with their hands up. Was this the end?

As I have already mentioned, the enemy had smashed through our neighbouring battalion and part of our platoon assigned to it. Their situation looked very bad. Without hesitating, the remaining units had regrouped to counter-attack. I was appointed a commander of one of these units. We felt the end was near as we gathered at our firing position. There was spoiled food in the quarters next to us, and our attention was drawn to a few packets of sweets.

The platoon commander and I were called to the company command post. There in the cellar, Waldemar was sat in front of his telephone switchboard, with a rather hopeless expression on his face. I told him about our new assault squad. He put a finger to his lips, laughed and whispered to me that the unit I had just told him about was supposed to break through the encirclement ring. It sounded unbelievable. In the meantime, my friend packed his military rucksack. Regretfully, he put a pair of women's shoes he wanted to send to his younger sister in the corner. With the present situation being so difficult, he knew he could not take them with him. He showed me a map with a 1:100,000 scale and explained in detail all stages of the planned exit.

It did not seem particularly easy, especially since we now knew that Schlang had not returned from his last reconnaissance. Our colleagues phoned Peter and Günter, who were sat with the rest of the battalion slowly preparing for the planned action. I could not hide the fact that the news about the upcoming operation moved me deeply. Günter and Peter could not understand my depression and tried to lift my spirits by messing about, but they were unsuccessful. We were very sorry that we were not going to break through together. Just as we were wishing each other good luck, happiness and promised mutual fidelity, the connection was broken and that was how our last conversation ended.

Together with my colleagues from the observation post, I returned to the mill to fine-tune the details of the operation. We had to leave the room we had furnished so without thinking, I smashed my three radios. However, I regretted this because they were supposed to decorate my future home. We left large stocks of food, tobacco and alcohol. It was not difficult for us to say goodbye to that place, because we hoped that our mission would be successful.

We gathered at the command post. At about 23.00, rations of brandy and tobacco were distributed before we carefully left the building. The Russians were conducting uninterrupted artillery fire, with bomber planes filling the sky. The final commands were given in a whisper. Suddenly, we saw a very tall man pushing through the crowd of civilians, demanding to speak to the commander. A face we all recognized emerged from beneath the tilted, dirty cap. It was our colleague, Hugo Schlang, who then proceeded to make his report in a brisk, military manner.

In the cellar of the command post, Hugo received a well-deserved distinction – a Leutnant's shoulder flashes – and joined our unit. We could not believe he was there. Faithful to the oath he had sworn as a soldier, he had carried out the order that had required superhuman abilities. Amazingly, our colleague Schlang had sneaked back and forth three times through the enemy lines, and as it turned out, he brought with him good news.

Our company moved forward slowly, led by Schlang and other officers. The city's streets were full of rubble. There was no house that had not suffered. Every telegraph pole stood crooked or was on the ground. We moved eastward to Fort Hake, passing burned cars and the bodies of dead horses as we went. We also passed small groups of soldiers. Roadside ditches to the left and right were full of the wounded, who all wanted to join us. At Fort Hake we were surprised to see two Russian officers. Walking past them, we heard them speaking German fluently, but I never found out the purpose of their visit.

After leaving the fort's ramparts, we entered a meadow and after walking through that, we reached the hill where the former large ammunition warehouse was located. We stopped to rest awhile. No one said a word, sticking constantly to the established rules, although it was difficult to march silently with our full equipment. I could not see Waldemar anywhere. We kept going, one after the other, evenly spaced. This was how we moved forward, but we soon descended into the well-known gravel pit. We climbed the crest of the ridge, crawling separately now at much larger intervals. We heard a whisper from the front ordering us to be vigilant; 150 metres to our left was a heavy Russian machine gun. We managed to pass by unnoticed. It is impossible to describe how much effort and nerve that moment cost us.

The ground was starting to get wet. We were moving very slowly by this stage, sometimes sinking knee-deep into the marshy terrain. The groans of people wading in the swamp could be heard from all sides. I hope I never again have to experience such a struggle against the forces of nature.

Large ammunition depots north of Fort IV 'Hake'.

Finally, we reached the forest. Were we saved? We looked back. On the horizon we could see a glow shining over the city, and we were surrounded by an unbelievable silence. And so began 16 February 1945; a date we will always remember. We moved on at a quick pace. Our designated destination was in the forest, east of Biedrusko, which was still about 30 km away. We covered about 4-6 km an hour, favoured by a bright moon that illuminated an exceptionally good map we had. My brave colleague Metzler - an Unteroffizier from Garmisch-Partenkirchen – and I knew the area quite well and for a while, we become the unit's vanguard. We were about twenty paces ahead and used Major Michel's[38] compass to guide us. Several times we came across the familiar boundaries of the Warthelager training ground. We rested for half an hour and looked southwest, where the sky from the fires in Poznań was still blood-red. We were overjoyed that we had broken through the encirclement and were still in one piece. At last we had the opportunity to congratulate our friend Schlang and shake his hand sincerely. We congratulated him

Major Michel on his horse during one of the 5th Infantry Cadet School parades. Poznań, 1943.

his promotion, but above all admired what his special mission had allowed us to achieve.

Dusk was falling. We looked at our watches and moved forward at a brisk pace. We made our way through the forest, sometimes overcoming ditches filled with water and other obstacles. At dawn we crossed the great highway; we could still see fresh traces of wheels and tracks on it. We started to look around for a thicket so that we could hide for the rest of the day, and after a while we found somewhere dark and overgrown. We first secured the area from all sides, before trying to prepare a bunker in the snow. We had hardly had any sleep and needed a well-earned rest, but despite our extreme fatigue, the cold bothered us so much that we could not fall asleep straight away. We ate a quick meal and then tried to sleep again. Most of us managed it eventually, but the bitter cold and our night-time experiences prevented us from having a solid rest. I think our feet were frostbitten. Once again, we thought about what awaited us.

In the meantime, our commanders (Major Michel and Hauptmann Heinemann) focussed on their detailed maps and worked out the rest of the route. We intended to reach the Oborniki forests in two days' time, where all units that had managed to break out were supposed to meet. Then, reformed into new groups we were to head to the Oder and cross it. What the finer details of this operation looked like, none of us knew. I held on to the hope that by some miracle I would meet Waldemar and the rest of my colleagues soon, believing that they had also managed to break out of the city. Back in the fortress of Poznań, we had fought and experienced tough times together, but this march would bring much brighter times for us.

Fate, however, had other plans.

The March North

We spent the day planning for our departure. We set off right after dark, setting the direction using the compass. The aim was to reach our destination, a section of a forest, by morning. Our commanders expected almost the impossible from us: leadership, reconnaissance, and securing the rear. My classmate, Hans Metzler, from Garmisch-Partenkirchen, and I were now at the vanguard.

Major Michel ordered a fast pace, even though the night was impenetrable. Almost blindly, we moved along the forest tracks, as our field of vision narrowed to just 1 metre. We were given an order that each of us should attach a piece of paper or white cloth to our backpack to show the way for the person following behind. We entered a thicket resembling a forest and after breaking through it, our path was blocked by a wide ditch filled with water. We had no option but to wade through it. We tried our best to cope with the challenge, even though the icy water was up to our knees.

After overcoming this obstacle, an arable field opened up in front of us. We waited in the furrow along its edge until the scouts had reached the forest wall on the opposite side. When they returned, we all tried to get up, but the clay and mud stuck to our shoes, paralyzing our every step. We reached the village around midnight and had a short rest in the square in front of the church. Metzler and I wanted to swap with someone else and no longer be at the front; we were tired of not only constantly looking for the route, but also directing the scouting parties. We wanted to be at the rear.

We sat with our backs against a roadside post and tried to take a nap. After a while we moved on, and the night was suddenly pitch black. Every now and then we checked whether we were in contact with those ahead. Suddenly, the seventh soldier ahead of me noticed that he could not see the man in front of him. The twelve of us stood at a crossroads, not knowing whether to go left or right. Our cries went unanswered. We fired flares and received a response, but we could not figure out what direction it came from. Slowly, we realized that we were on our own. As we were unable to determine our exact coordinates, we decided to wait for the upcoming day in a dense grove, where we were joined by six soldiers from another unit.

As dawn broke, we continued our march northwards through the woods, giving a wide berth to the towns we passed by. An accurate map with a scale of 1:100,000 helped us to orientate ourselves properly. At one point, a great 2-kilometre-long, empty space opened in front of us. The area was made up of meadows and fields, with a road running through the middle on which there was quite a lot of traffic. There were residential and farm buildings on both sides, and for a moment, we wondered how we were going to get through it. We decided to move along a roadside ditch and then cross it with a quick jump. We divided our unit into two groups, with me in the first. The ditch was quite high and provided us with good cover, plus the water in it was frozen. When we reached the road, we ran across. Despite our best efforts, the Poles had been watching us from their homes for a long time and as we ran madly across another meadow, they opened fire wildly from their skylights and windows. We all ran as fast as we could. Unfortunately, two of our colleagues were hit; their arms and legs shot through. We reached the edge of the forest and prepared to defend ourselves, fearing that we would be pursued. However, this did not happen. Those cowards hid in their windows and doors to hunt German soldiers undetected.

Then the second group set off. However, they were unlucky because as they were crossing the road, they met an oncoming Russian truck and there was a shootout. The driver was injured so his friend took his place and drove away like crazy. Just like us, our colleagues were shot at by Poles. After treating the wounded, we continued north. We made our way through the forests, avoiding the main trails, and in the afternoon of the same day (17 February), we reached the designated assembly point in the grove near Oborniki.

After a long search, we came across other units and waited together for nightfall. We asked the others about the 'Michel/ Heinemann' unit. Unfortunately, everyone's answer was the same; no one had seen them. We could not understand why they had not reached their destination. By the evening, we had to accept it and asked Hauptmann Spille[39] if he would let us join his group. As it turned out, Spille's battalion had suffered hardly any losses, and we admired their rich armaments. In addition to a small backpack, each soldier carried an MG ammunition belt and sidearm. The strike force of this group seemed to be very substantial. That evening, we all moved on together.

A group of German soldiers help each other to get ready to continue their march among the backwoods and winter scenery of the Eastern Front.

Commander Spille (already recognized at school as an outstanding tactician) led our unit perfectly. The next morning, we entered the moor. As most of the unit secured the area, the commander told us about his night-time tactical achievements. We had passed through a large town the previous night, but what we did not know was that a Soviet armoured unit with 150 tanks was stationed there. This experienced commander had led us through without us even noticing. He told us that sometimes you have to take a risk and bet everything on one card. He had done that and succeeded.

As it turned out, we unfortunately did not receive permission to continue the march together and were instead given a battalion officer with the rank of Oberleutnant. So, under his command, we continued on, although we would encounter Spille's unit several times along the way. The next day we met two Polish civilians who unfortunately reported our presence to the Soviet reconnaissance unit. There was an exchange of fire and the Russians retreated.

Carefully, we walked through the forested areas. Later, we came across swamps and marshes again, which were a serious obstacle. Luckily, a Polish civilian led us through along narrow paths known only to him. We realized that we had already reached the Noteć Valley, so to remain unnoticed, we stayed away from towns and villages, resting in groves and waiting for dusk. In the evening, we heard shooting coming from a nearby forest, which told us our colleagues on the other side had been ambushed.

We marched on. In the meantime, it had got very cold. We felt it acutely because we had not eaten anything warm for four days. We had to save food. I only had one can of soup left. I looked at my friend Hanitzsch from Dresden in disbelief – he had a backpack full of sweets, having convinced himself, and us, that sugar is the most nutritious meal.

We arrived at a forester's lodge at around 22.00, where we met the extraordinary hospitality of its Polish residents. We spend about an hour there, drinking coffee and eating our fill of cabbage. Warmed up and fed, we continued on our way. Some of us found the courage to ask for bread in a neighbouring village. However, they were met with hostility; the faces of the inhabitants expressed their feelings very clearly.

We were approaching the River Noteć, and even though we were still 3 kilometres away, we were already wondering if we would be able to cross it. We came across another forester's lodge, but this time it was deserted. After a quick reconnaissance, we took over the house, lighting fires in the ovens. Each of us was able to cook or fry something using the pots and pans. I warmed my soup and shared it with the senior private in our unit.

I was just scraping the leftovers out of my tin when the door opened suddenly and my friend Waldemar entered the room. He greeted me coolly, but cordially. I had not seen him since I left Poznań, and there he was, out of the blue, at the forester's lodge. Together with seven other soldiers, he had broken out westwards under the command of Oberleutnant Koppert (already a unit commander at our school).[40] In the general chaos, Waldemar had been admitted to their unit. The visitors brought six hens with them, which we cooked in a big laundry bucket. I ate a few plates of chicken stock and thanked fate for this extraordinary meeting.

We decided we would cross the Noteć together as a group, although we did not know how we would do it. We were on the edge of the forest, about 1 kilometre from the river, and decided we were going to build a raft by tying tree trunks together. However, a reconnaissance unit found a large boat in a nearby pond. It was so big that fourteen soldiers had to carry it. The road to the river was endless, so we shortened the route by walking through a nearby town, even managing to cross its main street unnoticed.

The riverbank dropped steeply, and as I was one of those at front, the weight of the boat crushed me to the ground. After a few steps we fell down, accompanied by loud curses and insults, and part of the group began to lose hope that the crossing would be a success.

After a while, we pulled ourselves together and started again. Thanks to a tremendous effort, we finally managed to launch the heavy, wet boat. There were about sixty of us in total. At this point, the river was between 150 and 200 metres wide, with a strong current. At 05.00, the first six men, including Waldemar and Oberleutnant Koppert, rowed towards the other bank, which took them some time.

Waldemar was about to head back but was clearly struggling. He wanted to carry on ahead but had given his word that he would come back for us and we would go together. We saw him hesitating and angrily cried out to him from our side of the river. The Oberleutnant promised him an Iron Cross First Class if he brought the boat back to us. I am convinced, dear Waldemar, that you and I both deserved more than the Iron Cross for what we had done in Poznań. And it was certainly not for this award that you returned to us with the boat. We said goodbye to our colleagues on the other side, hoping that we would meet again soon. I never saw them again.

Suddenly, two companions appeared. They had discovered a dam 500 metres away, meaning the rest of our group could cross the river without any problems. In the middle of the dam, however, was a lock keeper's house. Nevertheless, we decided to take the risk and crossed quickly to the other side. Our joy was indescribable. We had had so much trouble and struggled so hard, and now we had easily reached the other bank of the Noteć. Yet the rest of the river valley still had to be crossed.[41] Dawn was slowly breaking. A new day, 20 February, was beginning in that fateful year of 1945.

When most of the group wanted to get to the nearest village as soon as possible, the five of us (Waldemar, Ernst from Halle, Horst from Osnabruck, Kurt from Dresden and myself) decided to spend the day in a barn by the river. With difficulty, we opened the huge doors and prepared our beds in the hay. Waldemar shivered with cold and cursed under his breath; as we were crossing the ditch, he had miscalculated the distance and fallen knee-deep into the water.

The cold really took its toll on us that day. We locked the barn door and hid in the hay. Waldemar, still shivering, noticed several bags filled with clothes, which must have been hidden there by the owner for fear of the Russians stealing everything. My friend found a fabulous woman's coat with a large fur collar. After removing his soaked clothes, he was able to cover himself with it and keep warm. It was 08.00. We each looked for holes and gaps in the barn walls so as to observe the surrounding area. I could see the steep bank on the opposite side of the river. On the ridge of the slope, parallel to the flow of the river, was a road with a constant stream of traffic on it. We watched as an endless column of vehicles went by. They were not displaced Germans, however, but Russians. They wanted to make it clear who they were, so they fired and cheered nonstop. We also heard them singing, although it was partially drowned out by the roar of car engines. We held our breath as Russian infantry regiments marched past us. An infinite serpent of the enemy army passed before us, arranged in rows of four or six soldiers. At times we felt like the entire power of this great nation was marching before us. We looked at it all and wondered what else awaited us ahead.

It seemed increasingly unlikely that any further action would be successful. With such a large number of troops behind us, would we manage to get closer to the frontline unnoticed? We waited for nightfall. We knew that Black Sea Germans lived in the Czarnków district,[42] and so set off to try to reach one of their houses. Dogs were barking all around us, so we needed to be extra vigilant. When we finally met some of the natives, we could see that they were very restless. They were afraid of the Russians' arrival and asked us not to stay with them. However, they offered us plenty of bread with butter and lard, as well as some hot milk. But from house after house, everyone advised us to keep moving. We passed through the village and reached a secluded little manor house. After a long knock on the door, a frightened woman opened it, unable to believe that we were Germans. Even her little children were surprised to see us because so far only enemies had come to their home. We asked for some bread, only to find that the Russians had taken it. Instead, we got cold potatoes, milk and a piece of bacon. We accepted it all gladly. We had never been so blessed. We talked to the woman for a while longer. Her voice shone with the hope that the situation would soon change and the front would move in the opposite direction. She hugged her children close to her as she said goodbye to us. We thanked her for everything, wished her well, and left to take refuge in a nearby forest.

According to what we were told by the Germans we encountered, the frontline was now supposedly running through Stare Osieczno [Hochzeit].[43] We set the azimuth of the march to get to this area. We moved carefully to the east, along a fairly busy road which ran nearby, with telegraph lines on both sides. We passed a burned-out forester's lodge, proof that fierce fighting had taken place there recently. We found a lot of destroyed equipment and abandoned weapons. The lines of the trenches and the remains of firing positions indicated the likely route of the front.

We passed deserted houses and saw the familiar sight of furniture, clothes and laundry scattered all around. Hordes of Russians had passed this way, looting everything they considered of value. Whatever they deemed unworthy, they either destroyed or threw away. That night, we probably covered the greatest distance of the journey so far, all thanks to the scrupulous adherence to the compass. We wanted to go through a small town, but the barking of the dogs stopped us. We walked through a dark forest for a long time and when we reached a thicket, we noticed that dawn was appearing on the horizon. We discovered a small farm on a nearby hill and planned to stay there. To our great surprise, however, the door was opened by a German, who greeted us warmly. We were on the outskirts of Górnica [Gornitz],[44] where the majority of citizens were Poles. That is why we were so happy to meet the wonderful Sitz family. We saw a table set for breakfast, similar to those we remembered from peacetime, with white bread, butter and many different kinds of cold meats on it.

There was even hot milk steaming in the mugs. We ate and enjoyed our meal, feeling safe and secure under the Germans' care. The hosts enjoyed us being there and outdid themselves in terms of hospitality. They told us about the fierce battles that had taken place there and about their Polish neighbours. We were disappointed to hear that the front had shifted more to the west. But we also had a nice surprise after it turned out that the hosts had hidden a radio deep in their cellar. Despite the power supply there being very weak, we hoped that we would be able to pick up some reports in the afternoon, which would be very important to us.

The hours before dawn were spent talking and reminiscing. Our hosts offered us a large barn to sleep in. Equipped with blankets and pillows, we climbed the haystacks to finally get a good night's sleep. We felt safe because both the owners' sons watched over us. They woke us up at noon and invited us to a sumptuous dinner. We especially enjoyed the roast pork. However, we would soon find out that our stomachs were no longer used to such delicacies. At 14.00, we sat together in silence around the radio, listening carefully to the familiar words: 'The High Command of the Wehrmacht announces…' Unfortunately, the news from all fronts was not good. We listened for a while longer, then our hostess puts sausage sandwiches in our hands: our last meal of the day. As evening fell, tears ran down our faces as we bid farewell to this family of true German patriots.

We moved forward along forest paths and came across more burnt-out ruins of a forester's lodge. We searched it, as well as the nearby cellar, but found nothing of interest. We passed a small village on our right, then forded a wide stream and approached the local cemetery. It must have recently been a battlefield as we could see fresh trenches between the graves. We shook our heads with disgust and disapproval for those who failed to pay the proper respects to the dead. War was ruthless and was now being fought by savage nations. We moved on to look for accommodation for the upcoming day.

Something black and rectangular loomed before us on the horizon, which we mistakenly took for a shed. Our disappointment was great when it turned out to be a beech grove. Behind it ran a double-track railway embankment. We crossed it with the greatest care so as not to run into any checkpoints or patrols. We rested for a while and took out the rest of our sausage sandwiches, thinking back to our accommodation in Górnica. The terrain in front of us was becoming more and more diverse, which made it difficult for us to see ahead. In addition, there was no moon that night. We made our way through a dense pine forest to set up a camp in the middle of this wilderness and prepare our beds for the next day.

We fell asleep quickly but were woken at dawn by the noise of engines. We listened to where they were coming from and comparing our guesses with the map, we came to the conclusion that there was a major road about 2 kilometres away. We heard the sounds of vehicles all day long and become convinced that the Russians were transporting all their supplies along that road. At dusk, we headed towards the road along the shore of a large lake. It was the evening of 22 February. On both sides of the road were fields that provided no opportunity to hide. We ran in a tight group and jumped to the other side of the road, one by one. When we were a mere 50 metres behind it, a column of trucks came along. We pushed ourselves down firmly into the field furrows and watched as the vehicles loaded with sacks headed west.

Behind a small hill were some village buildings and we approached one of the houses that was further away from the others. As two of men stood guard next to the cars, we went inside hoping to ask for some bread. The woman standing in the kitchen opened her eyes wide in terror when she saw us there us in full gear. She put a finger to her lips and pointed another finger to the neighbouring room. Through the crack in the door, we could see two Russians sitting at the table, their faces lit by candlelight. We retreated silently, unnoticed. We did not risk trying to kill them, knowing that their companions were quartered in the nearby houses and would immediately come to the rescue at the sound of gunfire. We wondered what to do next. Three of us were opposed to entering any of the other houses, while the other two wanted to make one more attempt to get some bread. We moved on and soon saw a large lake connected to a second one by a fairly wide canal, which we could not cross. By circumventing this obstacle, our route was naturally much longer, and we deviated a bit from the established direction. At the northern tip of the lake was another busy road. We jumped into a roadside ditch and, under the cover of bushes, carried alongside, turning into a side lane after a while.

At the edge of the forest, we saw a terrible sight. A man and a woman – probably a married couple – from a group of refugees heading west had been brutally murdered by the Russians. Naked, with broken skulls and gouged-out eyes, they were victims of the 'chivalric' attitude of the warriors from the East. We shuddered at the sight of their bodies but could not stay there any longer. We had a short rest to establish our position in relation to the nearby mill. It appeared to be occupied by Poles, so after crossing a nearby stream, we changed direction and headed northwest.

We entered a forest and made our way with difficulty through its dense undergrowth to the next village. The houses, untouched by warfare, attracted our attention with their beauty and décor, almost encouraging us to enter. We could hear the sounds of cattle in the barns and the cars standing in the yard seem to be technically efficient. The buildings appeared to be inhabited. Looking around warily, we knocked on the first door and after waiting for a long time, a voice from inside finally asked what we wanted. Instead of the expected German we instead met a Russian, who, with increasing aggression, demanded explanations from us. We disappeared quickly, but realized that our search for compatriots in this area was becoming increasingly dangerous. The Russian had heard our voices and fired a few shots towards us. The only thing that worried us was whether he had alerted the rest of the village by doing so.

THE HUNTED

The frosts were slowly subsiding and the thaw was coming. It was becoming more and more difficult to move along the slippery forest paths. In the place where the edge of the forest met the lakeshore, we set up camp and lit a fire, hoping to warm up and take a nap. The next day was 23 February. In addition to the weather, cold and damp, we were suffering from hunger. We did not wait until the evening and after a few hours of sleep, at about 14.00, we moved on. So as not to risk crossing the road along the northern end of the great lake, we went around the reservoir from the south. We could see wheel tracks on the forest road and so headed deeper into the forest.

After passing the lake, we met another obstacle in the form of wide stream flowing out of it, cutting off our path to the north. After crossing an anti-tank ditch and several defensive lines, we reached a spacious concrete bunker. Its damaged equipment told us that it was a bunker belonging to the Pommern Stellung [Pomeranian Wall]. There was a wide road to the north of the fortification line. A part of the signpost was so far away that we could not see what was written on it. The nearest signpost showed the way to Człopa [Schloppe].

After confirming our coordinates on the map, we found that the busy road mentioned previously led to Drawno [Weddell], and so we decided we would head that way in the evening. In the meantime, we looked on the map for a forester's lodge in Pustelnia [Salmer Teerofen] village. We found its ruins near the bridge over the stream. Next to it was a garden full of carrots and a buried can of lard. Again, we had something to ease our hunger pains for a while as we waited in the bunker for night to fall. We moved north along the road, leaving it whenever we heard the slightest noise. We could smell smoke coming from a chimney in one of the buildings to the left. Not knowing whether it was a hut or a bunker, we gave it a wide berth just in case. We saw several traces of fierce fighting, stumbling over the corpses of soldiers from both sides, abandoned weapons,

57

Soldiers of the 1st Polish Army next to one of the blown-up concrete shelters of the Pomeranian Wall.

remnants of equipment. We passed a forest that had clearly been the target of massive artillery fire; the trees were broken and burned. Their treetops lay shattered on the ground.

Luckily, we could still proceed down the road. We heard music, singing and laughter coming from a remote village on the left. We stood in front of a large, fenced-in forest nursery. Using pliers he had brought from Poznań, Waldemar made a way through for us. It had begun to snow again. Because the forest roads had already softened after the thaw and were becoming almost impossible to walk on, rather discouraged by the adversities, we decided to rest for a few hours. Our mood was worsened by the fact that there were no places to hide, and we had left deep tracks in the snow. Our search for some form of shelter in the forest was futile, so we leaned together against a pine tree to sleep for a while. Waldemar lent me a piece of his rescued coat, but it was not enough to cover both of us. Soaked shoes and uneven ground prevented us from falling

Człopa in the 1930s.

asleep, so after a few hours we got up, shook off the snow and woke our three colleagues. Shivering with cold, we marched on to reach the frontline that night. We knew it must have been somewhere nearby because we heard increasingly clear machine gun fire and the thunder of artillery.

Attempts to Break through the Front

We deviated a bit from the proper course west and reached the vicinity of Drawno. The maps from the atlases at our disposal were inaccurate and did not allow us to orientate ourselves properly. Nevertheless, we had a feeling that we would soon find ourselves before the enemy, on the frontline.[45]

We walked west for many hours, using only a compass, and still following only icy forest paths. Suddenly, we noticed a light flickering among the trees. We approached cautiously and saw a group of Russian cavalrymen sitting around a campfire, engaged in a lively discussion. We stepped back slightly to avoid them but could see further light from campfires to the left and right, thus proving to us that we were finally close to our target. It was too dangerous to enter the village, so we turned left to descend into the dark, endless fields.

The campfires were behind us, but freshly built fortifications and firing stations told us that something was not quite right. Dawn was slowly breaking and we had to find somewhere to hide as soon as possible, even if it was just a barn or haystack. A square building on the hill emerged from the darkness. I made my way over quickly with a friend, hoping it was an empty shed. Instead, we realized it was a combat bunker, and on the way we passed many other fortifications. We stopped behind the building. In the lower part was a niche that provided shelter for the shooters, and as I was looking at it, talking quietly to my colleague, a Russian suddenly appeared. He did not put down his gun and proceeded to shout incomprehensible words at us. Apparently, because we were wearing Russian-looking fur hats, he had mistaken us for one of his own. It was then that I realized we were all in the middle of the enemy's main defensive line. I felt very nervous, knowing it would be reckless to kill the Russian now. When he went back into the bunker, we turned around and made our way back to our unit, slowly at first, then faster and faster. We tried to recover ourselves and drank some water from the trench. Taking into account the fact that we could come across enemy units at any time, we decided to go across the fields, heading west.

It was raining cats and dogs. The snow, which had been 20 cm deep not so long ago, was now turning into water and mud. We ran through the forest, only to find more firing positions at its western end. Further ahead we could see rushes, which we later realized were the banks of the Drawa, a small tributary of the Noteć.

It was now 19.00 and it seemed impossible for us to cross the river at that time. Our next decision bordered on madness. We paired up and decided to enter the enemy's freshly dug fortifications. Our devilish plan was extremely risky; Waldemar and I would climb into the large trench, the walls of which were gradually softening in the relentless rain. To protect us from the elements, we covered the trench with branches, although our provisional roof was rather leaky. We squatted down, took off our shoes and tried to wring out our socks to at least create the resemblance of being drier. It was getting very cold, and this would be the tenth day in a row where a hot meal was a real rarity. Our food supplies had dwindled almost to nothing. We only had a small chunk of bread, which we had found a few moments earlier in the Russian fortifications. We shared it between us and tried to get some sleep. It was not easy; rain, wet feet, hunger and sitting down are not conducive for resting. We took turns napping, thinking about our homeland, seeing our loved ones again, but above all about food. Time dragged on. Every time I looked at my watch, the previous hour seemed like an eternity. As daylight would reveal our position, we were doomed to endure our uncomfortable situation. Soon, we would find out this was not all we had to endure.

Exhausted, we closed our eyes before suddenly hearing the whistle of machine gun bullets over our heads. They passed extremely close by, and we woke up immediately. Our nerves and muscles tensed up as they did before when we fought with the Russians near Voronezh. With our rifles cocked ready between our legs, we waited to see the triumphant faces of the Russians appear from above. But nothing like that happened. Leaning out carefully from the trench, I spotted a Russian detachment of thirty men about 40 metres from the trench. They were firing left and right like crazy; I guessed in celebration.

We breathed a sigh of relief when they disappeared from view. If just one of them had guessed that eleven German officers in full uniform were lying in their trenches not far from them, not only would they have had another reason to celebrate that day, but they would certainly have received medals for catching us. We had survived, but still could not feel confident. Every now and then we saw more Russians passing by, often yelling or shooting into the air.

We could not wait for the evening. Frozen to the bone, hungry and soaked, we left the trench at about 19.00. Miraculously, I found a bucket full of plum marmalade in one of the firing stations. Without looking for a spoon, we greedily reached inside and ate it, licking and smacking our lips as if it were Christmas. We had managed to survive one more day. We remembered the words: 'Germany! Look how your officers are fighting!'

We left the rest of the precious marmalade in the bucket and moved on to find a way to cross the Drawa. We made our way through the thickets and rushes, wading knee-deep in water and mud. Finally, we reached the bank of the wide river. There was 20-30 metres of fast-flowing current between us and the other side. We wandered along the bank looking for a boat or a raft, losing a lot of time in the process.

We spotted a bridge 2 kilometres away, with cars regularly passing over it, their headlights shining in the dark. We decided to head in that direction and came across a railway line on the way, so we walked along the ditch by the embankment. We crept ahead and were only 10 metres from the bridge when we realized it was also a viaduct.[46] On the left we could see the road leading to it, although at that time not a single vehicle was visible. Everything was shrouded in the darkness of the night. There were no sounds. Slowly and carefully, we moved forward, believing that no one could see us. We were wrong.

Suddenly, we heard screaming from the Russians as the bullets from their machine guns rained down on us. We retreated quickly – that was our only thought. We hid under the pillars of the bridge and lay by the river, thanking God that we were all still together and that no one had been hurt. Bullets whizzed over our heads for a long time and the attack meant our first attempt to cross the river had failed. We had had enough adventures for one night. Crawling, we reached a riverside meadow in the morning and found a deserted barn full of straw. Without taking off our clothes and wet shoes, we buried ourselves in the straw and waited for the next evening to come. We were happy to be able to lie down and sleep. Our stomachs, naturally, rebelled, demanding normal food, and we slept very restlessly until nightfall.

I could see food in front of me in my mind's eye. I pushed those thoughts away, but they kept coming back. My dreams were filled with the most delicious dishes. It was a horrible feeling, very painful and my constant companion. We lay there hungry, waiting for evening. When it got dark, we set off with empty stomachs to look for a better way to cross the Drawa. The weather was changing again. It was still February, after all, so it started to snow and the temperature dropped. We were more visible to the enemy in all that ubiquitous whiteness. As time passed, we had no idea of what to do next.

Quarrels began. We reproached each other, with one person insulting another. Each of us had a better and more interesting idea and suggestion for how we would get out of the trap. Our nerves were stretched to the limit and consequently made life much more difficult for each other. We were still stood on the banks of the Drawa, not knowing what to do. Suddenly, we saw spheres of light high above, which we recognized as German flares. Judging by the enemy's movements, we knew we were about 1 kilometre from the enemy's most advanced bridgeheads,[47] and that the fortifications around us were just protective in nature.

We therefore came to the conclusion that we were stuck in the middle of the enemy's foreground, in front of a belt of fortifications. The next morning, our situation had not changed. We still had nothing to eat and so we looked again for the bucket of marmalade. After everyone had had a spoonful, we threw ourselves back in the straw. I felt as if my stomach had decided to consume itself. We prayed and wracked our brains for a way out. We were exhausted and knew that something had to happen to change our situation. If not, then what would become of us?

From our hiding place, we watched several Russians as they moved noisily around the area. The upcoming evening was to bring us our first success. Waldemar and I were almost ready to swim across the river, but we knew we would not be able to take our uniforms and weapons with us. Then we spotted a boat stuck in the reeds, which had probably been used by the Russians. Unfortunately, it was not moored close to the bank, but instead floated in a small lake next to the river. In any case, we immediately seized the opportunity. Now we all had a renewed strength. Forgetting about our hunger, we jumped to our feet to try to move the boat closer to the riverbank, where we had a better position to cross. The plan seemed simple, but it was anything but.

We bent under the boat's weight, feeling a searing pain in our shoulders. We had only managed to carry it for about 100 metres before some of us lost all our strength. The stronger colleagues scolded the weaker ones, urging them to try again. But it was no use. We were simply exhausted. We tried to push the boat into the water, but without success. We returned to the barn with what was left of our strength, while the two strongest among us stayed by the boat.

They returned after a few hours, their teeth chattering. Wet through, they told us the boat had capsized. Our last spark of hope had gone out.

The new day arrived and we had to tighten our belts again. Literally and figuratively. Some of us cried with hunger. I felt dizzy when I stood up, so I laid back down and once again began hallucinating about delicious food. We had no strength to think or talk, so just lay there and waited. In the evening, two of our colleagues found a bucket of potatoes from somewhere. We made a small fire in the barn and boiled them in the bucket. There were four pieces each and we ate them greedily, even the skins. This 'supper' made no difference. We had not had any warm food in our mouths for days, and the potatoes did nothing to fill the gap. Nevertheless, slightly refreshed (so we told ourselves), we made another attempt to lift the boat. Finally, after many attempts, we succeeded. At about midnight, the time to cross the river had arrived. Thank God we did it! At last, we had finally overcome this great obstacle. We were happy, but had no idea that this undertaking had not brought us even one step closer to our goal. We desperately wanted to break through to the other side of the frontline that night. Our hunger forced us to do so, and the health of one member of our group was already deteriorating. Having been wounded in Poznań, he had managed to survive to that point. A grenade fragment was still lodged in his right forearm and the wound was festering; his whole hand was terribly swollen. He also had a fever and his nerves were in shreds. In short, we had to reach our goal that night no matter what. We desperately wanted this to happen, but unfortunately, something completely different occurred. Something we could not have imagined in our wildest dreams.

In single file, with Waldemar at the front, we headed towards a hill overgrown with bushes. After a while we fell upon a dirt path and suddenly, from the darkness of the night, the outline of two figures emerged about 20 metres ahead of us. As they walked back and forth, we fell to the ground and wondered what those two sentries were guarding. A moment later, a cavalryman appeared and, following instructions from one of the guards, started to ride towards us. All of this happened in a split second.

The rider spurred his horse forward. Standing in front of us, he fired his gun. The horse reared, the rider shouted something, and both sentries threw themselves backwards. All hell broke loose. We tried to break through using the bushes as cover, but instead ran into a heavily manned Russian combat post. A terrible shootout began. We ran like crazy along the path we had come down, losing our caps on the way. The shooting slowly fell silent. Completely exhausted, we fell on the snow near the forest.

We were at most 100 metres from the Russians. We lay there and thought about the death that awaited us. However, it did not come. We looked at each other, but none of us knew what to do next. After a while, we realized grimly that our wounded colleague was not with us. Did they get him? Was it fate? Was that the end of his agony? We could not answer those questions. Some of the bullets had hit two of our companions. They had light scratches on their arms, but apart from that, nobody was hurt.

Instinctively, we climbed back into the boat on the Drawa and sailed it back to the other side of the river. Each of us dreamed of being able to lay down somewhere and close our eyes. We had gone through a lot that night. We had almost broken through. In our imagination, we saw ourselves somewhere in a German bunker being congratulated, enjoying the peace and looking forward to a holiday. But with one mighty blow, all our dreams had burst like soap bubbles, and all that remained was the harsh reality that a good friend had been taken away from us. Tormented, we fell on the straw. 'Germany! Look how your officers are fighting!'

Another day dawned. Our eyes were popping out of our skulls from headaches caused by hunger. Or at least that is how it felt. My stomach ached horribly. We were all so on edge that we decided to keep silent so as not to anger each other. I often woke up from the cold and would go to the nearest stream to quench my thirst, but it did not satisfy the hunger pains. Hours went by. If only we could fall into a deep sleep for a while... We were happy to see the daylight finally fade. We wanted to walk up the Drawa[48] until we found a ford or bridge to cross. In complete indifference, and abandoning caution, we groped our way forward. We heard shots nearby as we passed an artillery position. Two ponies were grazing in a small clearing. What a delicious roast they would make made of them. But which of us would have enough courage, not to mention strength, to kill and cook them? After walking for about 10 kilometres, we had had enough.

My God, were we really going starve to death? I wanted to scream out loud at the top of my voice in my helplessness. One of us pointed out that it was more difficult to survive if we were in a large group, so we decided to split into groups of five. My group wanted to lie on the straw as soon as possible, and we were soon joined by the other group, meaning we were one big unit once again. It was torture to lie on the straw and starve to death, but was still better than wandering in the woods. We all believed that our fate would change soon. I knew the feeling of hunger from my past actions in Russia and was aware that it is possible to survive eleven days without food, but that you cannot do anything during this time. The remaining hours of the night passed. We thought about our loved ones. If they knew what was happening to us and our situation, they would probably not be able to sleep either. It was good they did not know.

The next afternoon we often saw Russians nearby, hunting. They rowed on the Drawa and shot every bird they could see. Suddenly, we heard loud explosions. A group of Russians were catching fish by stunning them with hand grenades. They were only 100 metres from our hiding place. Coarse and armed to the teeth. They made us anxious as our own weaponry left much to be desired. We only had three guns and four machine guns. We watched the Russians constantly as they continued to throw grenades into the water and held our breath that they would not come any closer.

However, the Russians suddenly left the boat and started heading towards the barn. Our hearts leapt to our throats when we saw what weapons they were carrying. In a split second, we grabbed our rifles and jumped out on the opposite side of the building. We had to do so literally at the last minute because the enemy began to open deadly fire in our direction when they were around 30 metres away. By this time, however, we were already hiding in a nearby grove. They could not have seen us because we were not followed. With the last of our strength, we headed deeper into the forest. Suddenly, one of our men noticed a car driving towards us, as well as a group of fifteen to twenty Russians marching behind it. Instinctively, we threw ourselves to the ground and, thank God, they passed us by.

Using the compass, we returned to our planned direction of travel, after veering too far to the left before. After 100 metres or so, we saw another vehicle in front of us with three soldiers inside. Throwing ourselves to the ground again, we begged fate for a favour.

A group of German soldiers secretly making their way through the forest.

We survived again, but already knew that there were many enemy units stationed in the forest. After another 100 metres, we reached a thicket half a metre high and crouched down in the young pine wood. We suffered terribly all the time.

Completely exhausted from the chase of the last few hours, my body began to go on strike again. We frantically searched for something edible, but whenever I bowed my head, a blackness appeared in front of my eyes. In my hometown, it was sometimes said that hunger hurts, and I now knew the meaning of those words in all their terrible splendour. We were close to despair. In our terrible poverty we began to eat the moss growing on the saplings. There was plenty of it about and it did not matter if it was dry, the taste in your mouth was bitter and bland and was often mixed with sand. We tore it off the trees in handfuls. An older colleague, a veteran of the Great War and a former Freikorps[49] soldier, broke off the bark of the larger pines. Using a knife, he scraped off its inner layer and chewed it. Each time he discovered anew that it was impossible to swallow. 'Germany! Look how your officers are fighting!'

Thank God it was evening and we could move on. We wanted to try to walk east for about 10 kilometres, then turn north and risk breaking through the frontline again. The most important thing was to get away from that dangerous area. Hunger meant that our ability to concentrate decreased, and we often strayed from the route. We could not find proper forest paths and trails, but in the middle of the wood we found an abandoned barracks. We searched the empty rooms for something to eat, but in vain. A light was on in one of the buildings and we heard some loud shouts. Once again, we had to dodge and go around the area so as not to fall into the hands of our 'neighbours from across the border'. During those dark nights we often imagined what would happen if we collided with one of the Russian troops. How often did we see death before our eyes.

After crossing a main road and a railway line, we came out into the open. We had to cross a huge area of meadows and fields to reach the forest visible in the distance. It was getting warmer and the snow had melted again, but the conditions in the fields were not in our favour. We were ankle-deep in mud, which clung to our shoes so that walking become a torment. Sometimes we would stumble and fall. What we had to do that night was unimaginable. There were puddles of melted snow and rain here and there, and we drank the dirty water greedily, without thinking about any potential infections.

We entered a potato field and each of us dug up a few for himself. Those who had knives peeled them, but I just rubbed them with the edge of my coat and tried to bite them. I had never thought raw potatoes could taste like that. I chewed and swallowed them again and again, without stopping. But our enthusiasm vanished as soon as it had appeared. You cannot eat a great deal that way. At one point I even began to wonder what was better: potatoes or moss.

About midnight, we made our way through more bushes. We heard the sound of engines running in front of us, which forced us to be especially careful. Suddenly, a row of lights flashed between the pines. We crept ahead slowly and saw two tanks standing 30 metres ahead. The crews were busy working on the engines and did not look our way at all. We remain unseen and, having moved away a bit, decided to take a short break. If we had not been so hungry, we would probably have fallen asleep straight away. But danger lurked everywhere, so we could not let down our guard. The moon rose and illuminated our faces. I think it was a full moon. We looked at each other. My God, how much older we all looked: dirty, unshaven, with sunken cheeks and dark circles under eyes. We groped on, blindly. Everything in us was weak and futile, 'but our faith was unique'. It is faith that makes us do superhuman things. Faith, which Lazarus' sister, Martha, said could 'move mountains'.

We were heading towards a bigger town and the barking of the dogs made us worried that we would be noticed. We could see the Russians' positions on the shore of a great lake, while the scene around them was the same as usual: hay and straw in the trenches, with rubbish, pots, laundry and clothes all scattered around. We checked every foxhole hoping to find a small piece of dry bread. But hope, as they say, remains the mother of all fools. We moved along the road, alternating between the left or right roadside ditch so that if the enemy discovered us, we would be able to run straight to the forest. We passed the decomposing bodies of horses, burned-out vehicles, abandoned ammunition and artillery guns. We found a bucket of sourdough next to a destroyed car. We asked one in our unit – a cook – if it was edible. We tried, but it turned out to be rancid and I could not swallow more than one portion. I did not want to ruin my stomach. The most important thing for all of us was not to get sick. There was also a dead piglet in the trench. We tried to cut it open, but the meat already smelled. With sadness, we knew we had to leave it if we did not want to poison ourselves.

After a while we came to a crossroads. A signpost read 'Neu-Körtnitz [Nowa Korytnica] 9'. Nine kilometres to the next town? Could we manage that? We did a quick calculation to see if we could get there before dawn. We would have to make an effort, and some of us did not want to go, preferring instead to stay in the woods rather than walk that far. But perhaps at the end of the day's wandering we would find some kind people or a barn full of hay? We decided to move on. Our spirit was willing, but the flesh was weak. After a while we had to stop to rest. I sat on a roadside post and held my heavy head in my hands. After a few minutes, we marched stubbornly ahead again.

How would it all end? None of us had enough courage to voice our worst fears aloud. We kept going. Not like before, in tight formation so as to be able to fend off a possible attack. Now we were rather more like a haphazard jumble of tired warriors. The soldier in front of me stumbled over something in the middle of the road between the clothes, mattresses and household appliances. That 'something' was a large can of food. He called us over to him and held out an open 3-pound can of luncheon meat. We shared it among us, and with trembling hands took out its contents one by one. After distributing the meat, when each of us had a piece as big as his fist, my first reflection was that God would never abandon a decent German in need after all.

At this time all our thoughts became, in a sense, a thanksgiving prayer. I knew that each of us was thanking Providence in words or in our hearts. After two weeks of hunger, we told ourselves that we would be strong and refreshed again after this nutritious snack of a bit of meat and fat. I had often experienced something similar in Russia, especially during the guerrilla war of exhaustion near the Romanian border. Whenever we lost our last hope, when further fighting made no sense, it was precisely then – and not before – when God would appear and help us. He always chose that moment for us to feel his helping hand.

A little further on, one of us found a piece of pork fat wrapped in a torn shirt. We divided it piece by piece and marched briskly onwards in a joyful mood. We were only 2 kilometres away from our desired goal when I found a dead and dismembered pig lying in a sack by the road. It must have weighed about 30 kilos and although the meat was not fresh and already smelled a bit, we managed to cut a few large chunks out of it. We approached a village with the intention of cooking the pork (perhaps with some potatoes). I cut myself a piece of lard and a little fat from the belly and rump to render.

Deep, fresh wheel marks on the road indicated to us that we were now on the enemy's main supply route. Our suspicion was confirmed by a newly built wooden bridge on the outskirts of the village. The sight in front of us shocked us too: of the twenty houses we counted, none had survived. They had all been burned or demolished. We had finally arrived at the place we had such high hopes of, and we were bitterly disappointed. The whole of the main street was covered with household appliances, mattresses and clothes. A few of our men arranged a small, stable-like building with a straw-lined floor for sleeping. Waldemar was particularly keen on the idea of camping there. I was against it because the tracks we had seen earlier testified to the increased traffic in the area, which had great implications for us. After all, we could not fall asleep in a place where the Russians would pass by within 10 metres at any moment.

With my companion from Gelsenkirchen, we took a trip among the ruins of the village. At the opposite end we found a bigger, not too damaged house, which had probably belonged to a forester.

There were two Wehrmacht cars in the yard, but they looked damaged. Their windshields were broken. We went through the individual rooms, but everything that had once made up the décor of this six-roomed house had been smashed to smithereens. The contents of chests and cabinets were scattered all around. My attention was drawn to the once-rich bookcase. On the tables and windowsills were dry and mouldy pieces of bread. After a long search, we collected a whole bag of these scraps. A half-empty jar of currant jam tasted good despite the layer of mould on it. We also found some salt, but nothing else. There was straw in all of the corners, and you could see that the Russians had stayed there for the night. You could almost break down looking at this lost legacy of proud Germans. But this was war. There was no time for sentiment. The linen and bedding closets had been used by the Russians as a toilet. It blew our minds. How did these savages think they could prove their cultural superiority to us Germans?[50]

The kitchen door opened with difficulty. To our surprise, in the middle of all that mess stood a huge bull, weighing at least 750 kilos, which stared at us, wildly. What the Russians had done there is indescribable. We searched the cellar looking for preserves, but the jars had all disappeared with the enemy. Finally, we saw the cars. The tyres were intact, and the engines appeared to be in good working order. 'If we had fuel', my colleague said, 'we could drive them away'. Joyfully greeted by our waiting companions, we distributed the bread we had found. Everyone was chewing and munching loudly. My God, how wonderful it was to finally have something hard to bite on. It was good that none of our relatives could see how we greedily ate the remains of food leftover by the Russians.

We decided to camp in a nearby forest. The others followed with reluctance and gloomy faces, not yet realizing how good the decision would turn out to be. About 500 metres from the village, we sat down in the forest. We lit a fire, quickly set the pan, and after a while the first steaks started to sizzle. Waldemar and another friend decided to return to the village to bring some potatoes from the cellar. In the meantime, our cook turned the steaks with professional expertise. We sat around and enjoyed our first warm meal for days, although unfortunately, the meat remained undercooked.

Suddenly, we heard the noise of machine guns coming from the village. We saw a group of Russians running along the street, shouting and shooting. Our friends were nowhere to be seen. In a flash we put out the fire, laced our backpacks and, in a mad rush, ran deep into the forest. In those days, how often did I think about the title of that famous book, *The Hunted*?[51] After a while, the shooting stopped. Our 'potato pickers' ran down the left-hand side of the village, breathing heavily. It was vital we all kept moving, so we all ran together about 3 kilometres, stopping in a small pine grove. Exhausted, we fell onto the moss as our friends told us what had happened to them. They had just been coming out of the cellar, with bags full of potatoes, when a dozen Russians appeared out of nowhere 20 metres ahead of them. Everyone was surprised. Before the shooting began, both our heroes dodged out of the way and ran to the side. The enemy ran after them, firing like crazy, but they only managed to hit a coat sleeve.

After a relative period of calm, I approached my friend from Gelsenkirchen and together we considered the words he had spoken not half an hour before in the forester's lodge: 'Come on, Hans, let's get out of here. I have this weird feeling I think we need to run.' We were not superstitious, but it seemed we had a guardian angel accompanying us again. It turned out that the cars parked in the yard, which we had examined so thoroughly, belonged to the Russians. As we were rummaging around the house, they were sleeping next door in the stable. We could not believe it and were full of gratitude to whoever it was who had guided us.

Around noon, we were awoken by the sound of engines coming close by. Our scout left on watch later said that two cars full of Russians had driven past our hideout. We felt constant gratitude. I tried to fall asleep in the grove, taking off my coat to use as a blanket, but it started to rain. What would be next?

Between the village and the grove was a hunting platform belonging a previous forester. We had noticed it before because, unlike the others we had seen, it had a roof. It had a small door and windows. We climbed into it (all except for Ernst from Halle, who was very careful in such situations. I am unsure why). The construction provided shelter for no more than two people. There were ten of us, but at least we would not freeze in that crush. We did not speak, each of us thinking only about the morning's events.

We waited for evening and our next hike, but in the meantime, it started to snow again. An icy wind penetrated the gaps of the platform, and I pressed myself harder against my friends. The hunger also took its toll. We tried to nap so that we would be awake for the evening, but it was not easy at all as it was impossible to lie down in a space where ten people could barely fit. There were two boards under the platform, so we lifted them upstairs and built a mezzanine. Now we could lie down on two levels. It was hard to stretch our legs, but at least we could lie down. My legs were against the door, which could not be closed. I think they were frostbitten, and this made falling asleep even more difficult.

Before our departure the next day, to fight our hunger we decided to roast a piece of meat we had saved after escaping from the Russians. We spent the rest of the day eating our meal in a small tree house, 10 metres above the ground. Our hunger and discomfort made us all resent each other, although we all shared the same fate together. To take away bad thoughts, we often prayed: 'Dear God, let us make it through to the evening.'

Our time was coming. We covered a large section of the route to the north. It was harder to find our way in the darkness and so we decided to stop in the middle of a forest to light a fire and roast a piece of pork in a small pan. We collected the firewood, but it was so wet we could not light it. Some of us were so discouraged that they refused to go on. I felt sad because I did want to return to the platform to spend the rest of the night there. We looked around and searched the abandoned Russian combat posts. Here and there we managed to come across some bread, which was soggy with snow and rain: a symbolic tribute to our stomachs.

Two of our companions discovered an extremely dense and dark pine grove nearby. We went deep into it to try to light a fire again and roast the meat. This was reckless on our part, but hunger often drives people to do things that are beyond reason. This time, however, we succeeded, and the meat sizzled in the pan. After a while, each of us was holding a piece of it in our hands, treating it like a gift from heaven. Although it was not salty, we were still so grateful for it from the bottom of our hearts. As well as the steaks, we prepared a soup made of melted snow and fat, which was also bland and tasteless, but at least it was warm and good for our stomachs. We ate and drank, taking a piece of meat with us for the road. In my backpack I discovered half a kilo of pork fat, which I melted together with the bacon.

We decided to break through northwards to finally break the frontline the next night. We stopped for a while at the edge of a forest. In the sky above us – almost within arm's reach – we saw rising German and Russian balls of light. The machine gun fire was so loud we thought we could run right there. But it was all just an illusion of light and sound.

The Hunted

We left at about 19.00. Our new map had a scale five times smaller than the previous one and was not as accurate, but we had already covered both railway lines marked on it. We saw more and more flares rising above us, which we defined as German or Russian by their colours. The roar of the machine guns was getting closer and closer. A farm was on fire somewhere in the distance. We felt exceptionally strong and had a firm resolve to carry out our plan that night. We marched eastwards along a wide road, our intention being to break through the line near Mirosławiec [Markisch-Friedland].

As it happened in those nightly marches, Waldemar and I took turns leading the group, and now I was leading the squad for a long stretch of the route. I often checked the direction with a compass, constantly looking from left to right. I wished I could see through the darkness ahead. Sometimes I even had dark spots in front of my eyes. Normally, one would talk about exhaustion in such cases, but I did not allow myself to think about things like that.

We were desperate to reach the German defensive lines that night, so we moved forward with determination. I shyly imagined being welcomed by our own troops, dreaming that they would lead us to the company command post. Then there would be an interrogation with the commander, admission to the division, and so on. I thought about the all-encompassing sense of security with particular delight. It would be wonderful! I even dared to think about a well-deserved holiday in my homeland. Oh, my God, I would finally see my loved ones again.

Two figures emerged from the darkness in front of me, making me forget about all those beautiful dreams. We needed to jump back into the bushes on the left. The men following me did not notice the impending obstacle at all, only finding out about it when we were in the middle of the grove. Two of us sneaked up to the road and saw two armed Russians patrolling a section of it. Thank God we had not run into them because it could have ended badly. We wondered for a moment whether it would be better to kill them both, but since we had absolutely no idea how many enemy soldiers there were nearby, we gave up the idea.

It had been snowing steadily for two hours. The pine branches that shielded us bent under its weight. We moved forward, low to the ground. The snow fell under our collars, and we became increasingly soaked. Our trousers were completely wet, and our hands were like ice, but we continued on. Every now and then we had to pull out the compass to check our direction. The grove seemed to be endless. We had been walking in the snow for hours. We made our way through the bushes and entered a tall forest. I was horrified to see that despite our increased caution, we had left deep tracks behind us. I hoped they

IS-2 tanks from the 4th Heavy Tank Regiment, 1st Polish Army, occupy Mirosławiec, which was fought over between 9-10 February 1945.

would not be our ruin! We had to cross telephone lines many times in the fields, which made us think we were close to some command post. We increased our vigilance, but at one point decided to take a short break in the forest. A terrible blizzard had begun, which was so thick that we had to close our eyes and hide under the pines. So as not to break down, we did not analyse our position. The balls of light in the sky seemed to be getting bigger, and the machine gun fire was getting louder. We had to break through that night at any cost. Our decision had been made and we kept the faith that we would succeed.

Once again, we had open territory to overcome. We did not feel particularly confident, because we knew that our grey figures stood out against the background of the white fields. We could see some buildings on the slope of a hill in front of us and decided to go around them and turn right. I had the impression that there were some sounds coming from the forest ahead and told my colleagues about it. We turned right again and suddenly Waldemar noticed several figures moving behind us. I also saw a man bending over the ground. We tried to reach the forest to take a short break there, suspecting that we were being chased by Russians, who kept calling out: 'Tracks, tracks! Look!'

It was 23.55. We stood up and then fell down. Again and again. We wanted to avoid being seen at all costs. We were afraid that the Russians would open fire on us, which would inevitably alert the remaining units stationed in the area. If that happened, our attempt to break through the line would be thwarted. We could only breath freely in the nearby juniper bushes. It was now midnight. The snow was slowing down and we could see the first stars in the sky. We tried to go on. Everything looked so peaceful and safe, but as it turned out, this was just an illusion.

We could see barracks in the forest to our right. Previously they had been camp services quarters but were now probably Russian supply warehouses. On the road leading up to the buildings were fresh, deep tyre tracks. We sneaked past with the upmost caution, passing many fortification systems along the way, which we realized were part of the Pomeranian Wall.[52] Soon, we reached the road to Mirosławiec.

After leaving the forest, more open territory opened up in front of us again, and we had to make a detour to get around it somehow. As we moved forward, I had the growing feeling that we were being watched. I was not sure from which side, but the feeling not only stayed with me, but grew stronger and stronger. We walked through three forest clearings, and in the last one, the melting snow and rain had formed a small puddle. We greedily drink the clayey water and filled our canteens, discussing what to do next. I suggested that someone replace me in the lead as I would rather someone else took over the responsibility for our unit. I joked about being engaged and wanting to live to see my wedding day, but all the other 'bachelors' remained silent. I realized I would be unable to convince any of them and I would not turn my back on them, so I tossed the gun over my shoulder and took the lead once more. We continued on.

I led the group through the middle of the clearing towards the nearest forest wall. The moon rose and illuminated our ghostly figures against the white, empty space around us. We had about another 50 metres left to reach safety when all hell broke loose. White and red flares lit up the sky above us and shots were fired from behind, first from just two or three rifles, before more joined in. The fear took our breath away. We ran like crazy, as fast as we could, the bullets whizzing past our ears. On both sides flares fell and faded out with a loud hiss. We ran into the forest, but the firing did not stop. Pieces of wood and branches fell on our heads. As I ran, I did not even look at my friends out of the corner of my eye. I did not know if any of them stumbled, fell, or died. At times like that a man becomes a ruthless egotist. We kept going through the forest for a few hundred metres, before silence finally fell.

Panting, we fell onto the frozen snow with the last of our strength. I could hardly breath and felt a cold sweat running down my forehead. I closed my eyes, trying not to think about anything except lying there, but that moment did not last very long. I heard a heart-rendering cry from our youngest colleague: 'My thumb, my thumb!'. Blood was flowing uncontrollably from his right hand and his finger was hanging by the tendons. We treated him quickly, but he remained in shock, running frantically back and forth shouting something incomprehensible about breaking the frontline. Meanwhile, another one of our colleagues was trying to take off his left shoe: he had been hit in the heel.

Our cook lay unconscious next to me, and I lost my mind looking at it all. Should I have thanked God for saving me? Should I have put my hands together and prayed? Would that have been selfish and completely unchristian? I do not know. I was simply unable to gather my thoughts. Next to me, a friend from Wuppertal was leaning against a tree. Suddenly, he fell to the ground and begged us for help in a tearful voice. We picked him up and he pointed behind him. We tore off his coat and uniform. His underclothes were soaked with blood and I felt sick as we took them off. I tried to pull myself together and not faint. The sight was terrible. His back was all red and blood was flowing from the wound next to his spine. We put gauze on it and covered it with a bandage, but he fell to the ground. 'Leave me.' Those were his last words. I had never felt so helpless. Should we have stayed with our wounded friends and let them capture all of us early the next morning? I could not decide. Waldemar told me that we needed to move on. We lay together in the snow for a while, looking at the swaying tops of the pines and the stars shining between them. 'Germany! Look how your officers are fighting!' My friend got up and I stood beside him. We hesitated for a moment before walking a few steps away from the others, where we were joined by three of our friends. Four injured colleagues were left behind as we slowly moved on.

We had already gone quite a way when we heard the sound of gunfire. My God! May they rest in peace. In silence, more depressed than ever, we followed the tracks we had made ourselves not so long before. We were heading backwards, but I did not know where to. We had taken a risk and put everything on the line. We had done everything to break through and had made a great sacrifice. It was not the reality we had dreamed of.

Maybe an hour had passed when we decided to stop for a rest at the hunting platform. Unfortunately, it was even colder up there. An icy east wind blew through the cracks and ultimately, we had to surrender that place, preferring instead to warm up by walking. I felt like I was about to burst into tears. My completely soaked feet had become blocks of ice. We covered about 10 kilometres, most of the time following our own footsteps. We wondered how long we would have to go, but no one knew the answer to that question.

I argued a little with Waldemar. He wanted to go back to the family from Gornitz, who had welcomed us so warmly that night. I dreamed about my own home. I wanted to make another attempt to break through the lines that night, but I knew that was madness given our state of mind and the condition of our bodies. However, I tried to convince Waldemar that going back made no sense, that we could not give up because we owed it to our loved ones. I wanted to be able to tell my family that I had tried everything in my power to reach them and that I did not break down. However, I would not blame fate if that were never to happen.

It was still snowing so heavily that we had to squint our eyes. Our biggest worry, however, were the footprints we were leaving behind. The snow did not cover them completely. It was approaching 06.00, and the dawn of 3 March was breaking. We were exhausted and had to stop every now and again. We tried to stick to the compass and head southeast. I was happy to stick to the first part of the direction but would resist the second part with all my might; I did not want to head east.

We entered the road leading to the village of Biały Zdrój [Balster] and had been heading towards it for some time when, half a kilometre away, we saw the ruins of a forester's lodge.[53] There were three bunkers right next to it, their doors and windows reminding us of small summer cottages. Inside we found bunks and mattresses, but there was no stove. We knew that hiding there was a big risk, especially since they were on the main road and very close to the village. However, we were frozen and as resigned to our fate as only those who are forsaken by Providence can be. Our only wish at that point was to lie down, close our eyes, and forget about all the depressing things that had happened to us for a few hours. Being careful, we set up a sentry system and swapped every half hour, although the changes would always occur exactly as our feet were starting to warm up.

We watched the village carefully. There was only smoke from two chimneys, which potentially indicated that there were still a few inhabitants there. A few children were playing by the road, and we could see cars coming and going with belongings. We guessed it was the Russians plundering the village. We searched all the nearby bunkers, with our colleague from Osnabrück finding half a loaf of bread in one of them. It had been softened so much by the snow and rain that we did not eat it. My insides were starting to fail and I could feel a growing pain in my stomach and intestines. I guessed it was the result of eating the fatty pork and not knowing how old the meat was.

Our sleep, interrupted by the necessity of changing the guard, did not give us a proper rest. Going outside constantly was not good for our health, either. By the evening, I was unable to stand on my feet. I had a fever and so lay down on a bunk and let myself be covered with everything we had. I needed to sweat it out so that I would not get sick. If only my feet would dry out. Meanwhile, my friends brought bricks to build a small hearth. We lit a fire but kept the door slightly open. This was certainly very reckless because, as I have mentioned before, we were very close to the village; the bunkers were by the road, and wet wood produces much thicker smoke. We told ourselves that we could feel the warmth from the fire, hoping that at the same time no one would notice the light from behind the half-opened door.

Waldemar brough some snow in a mug then melted it and gave me some hot water to drink. What an incredible feeling! I was so grateful to him for that. The others tried to dry out the bread, but I did not want to eat anything at that moment. I just wanted to rest and not think of anything. That night, my condition deteriorated. I began shivering and groaning loudly, preventing the others from being able to rest. I just wanted to make it through the night. Luckily, I felt a little better in the morning. I wanted to get up but had a terrible headache, so I lay down and slept all day. We moved on in the late afternoon of 4 March.

I moved with great difficulty. My shoes and socks were dry, but I was very weak and all my limbs hurt. After a meal consisting only of a slice of toasted bread, I tried to keep up with the others but after a few hundred metres, I noticed it was becoming too difficult for me. I wanted to fall down where I was and go to asleep. However, that meant I would be left alone to die, so I pulled myself together with what remained of my strength. The snow continued to fall. I had lost my hat so instead tied a scarf with red and white flowers around my head, but it got wet very quickly. We had to go lower, into a little valley, where there was a stream 2 metres wide in the middle.[54] There was no bridge or footbridge in sight, although a tree had been thrown across at one point. It was very narrow, only a few centimetres thick, but we had lost a lot of weight and were very thin so were able to walk across it to the other side, helping each other as we went.

We walked through a tall, dense forest. It was difficult to compare the route with the compass because visibility was limited to 5 metres. We crossed the railway embankment (which we would later learn was the line to Wałcz [Deutsch Krone]), and its condition showed that trains ran on it every day. Beyond was a wide swamp. Just when we thought we had overcome it, we suddenly sank very deep. I was limping up to my knees, unable to move. My friends had to turn around to help me as I could not get out of it myself. After breaking free of the quagmire, we tried to reach the cluster of nearby houses.

Our shoes squeaked and squelched with every step. 'Let's just keep going,' we repeated constantly, so as not to give in to doubt.

Rather boldly, we approached the first farm.[55] It was uninhabited, but its condition showed that our enemy had wreaked the same vengeance on it as usual. All the equipment had been smashed into the tiniest pieces. The entire floor of the house was covered in half a metre of rubble, shells, and torn clothing. In the crack of a large broken mirror was a piece of bread. We could not believe it. There we were starving to death and those wild beasts were breaking mirrors by throwing bread at them. The broken arm of a courtyard pump was stuck deep into the wardrobe door. We could clearly see what kind of games the Russians liked. We also had a clear picture of their culture. One of my colleagues found the remains of a sausage, while another found a few onions. I was happy to pull a can out of the rubble containing sugar beet syrup. We shared our spoils, eating them with the rest of the bread we still had left. I was also happy to find a hat, which I put on instead of the scarf. My friend from Osnabrück tried on a large fur hat. He looked impressive in it. Alongside his camouflage uniform, it made him look like a Russian from a distance.

The sounds of dogs barking and the clang of opening gates warned us against approaching any of the other houses. We gave up any further searches, deciding that we did not fancy potentially running into the enemy, especially since there were so few of us left. We soon found ourselves stood in front of the fence surrounding the forest nursery and again, the pliers belonging to the telephonist from Poznań (Waldemar), proved themselves useful. We sneaked through the fence and reached a large manor house which, we would later find out, was called the Brodzce [Kummant] forester's lodge. The forestry workers' huts behind had been burned down, but the great house, stables and farm buildings remained intact. We felt apprehensive as we approached the barnyard because we could see cows standing in the barns. We thought the Russians must be there because civilians in those parts certainly did not have any farm animals. Our attention was also drawn to the telephone lines coming from the side of the manor house. We passed around the entire farmyard and from there looked back once more from a distance, admiring this wonderfully situated estate. A large lake at the front gave it a truly majestic character. We refreshed ourselves with water and then continued our march southeast.

We entered a forest track and followed it for quite some time. At a fork in the road, we stopped to consider whether to go down a wide, cobbled street. The route was not quite in line with our chosen direction, but we told ourselves that we could move a lot faster by walking on such a surface. Unfortunately, we soon came across an obstacle in the form of an anti-tank ditch, which cut across our trail. Next to it was a small plaque with a skull drawn on it. We walked around the ditch, but after a few hundred metres, we once again found ourselves in front of barbed wire fences built in a hurry from a huge number of pine logs. We avoided them, regardless of the danger. There were lots of foxholes and trenches in the forest surrounding the great Lake Sitno [Zientefier-See], which had previously been staffed with our troops, and then the Russians.

We slowly looked around for shelter for the coming day. Our shoes were still dripping with swamp water and our feet were frostbitten. Meanwhile, our trousers had stiffened from the frost and looked like metal pipes. Each of our steps was accompanied by a crunching sound. Any noise we made could bring us misfortune, but despite warning each other, we had no influence on the situation in any way.

An Unusual Meeting

Two parallel branches, each 5 metres wide, flowed out of the lake. We crossed them on a surviving bridge and then followed the shore southwards.[56] We tried to find some shelter, hoping to dry our shoes and socks. My friend from Osnabrück was leading us and after some time, on the opposite bank [of the River Płociczna], he noticed the roof of a house protruding over the white horizon. We hoped this could be somewhere we would be able to rest.

We reached the sluice and crossed it. In case of any surprises, we set up a general action plan and semi-confidently entered the farmyard.[57] First, we looked into the outbuildings, where to our great astonishment we found some chickens. There were nine of them in total. We concluded that there must have been people living nearby, but we could not see or hear anyone. Carefully, we approached the two-storey house. The rooms inside presented the same, familiar sight. However, the extent of damage here was greater than elsewhere, although the reason for this may have been the torn uniform we saw lying on the floor. We could not open the living room door as it had been blocked with a sofa. However, when we finally managed to force it open, two huge grunting pigs appeared before our astonished eyes. They fled, squealing and stumbling over rags and bed springs that stuck out everywhere. Someone had to have been feeding them, and we wondered who had taken care of them and shut them in the room.

In the meantime, Waldemar lit a fire in the kitchen stove and we were finally able to take off our wet trousers. We looked for food and found potatoes in the cellar. We cut the heads off three hens and plucked them, and there were soon wonderful smells coming from the kitchen. We had to hurry, knowing that we had to extinguish the fire before dawn so that the smoke from the chimney did not betray us. I had volunteered to be the cook, so was frantically trying to prepare the roast chicken in a gravy and nutritious broth. Unfortunately, I made a mistake and the soup was oversalted. Everyone was disappointed. I would remember that for a long time and be forced to endure to mockery of my comrades. Still, the chicken in a roux sauce was delicious.

As the youngest in our group, our colleague from Osnabrück was tasked with bringing water from a stream using buckets and watering cans, cursing under his breath as we urged him to go and fetch more. But it was for a good cause, and he did it dutifully. After a while he came back and excitedly pointed us to a shed at the edge of the forest, where he believed there were Russians staying.

We immediately took up positions in the windows and prepared to defend ourselves. But there was nothing but silence. Our dear friend Horst bravely moved towards the shed, taking only a gun with him. In his hat and winter uniform, he could certainly pass for a Russian. Suddenly, we heard the screams and cries of women, who emerged from behind the buildings and ran away in panic towards the forest. Our companion heard German words and urged them to stop. Suffice to say it was a great surprise for both sides! The women followed our friend into the house. A new, remarkable day had come. The unforgettable 5 March 1945 – a day of an extraordinary meeting. The women embraced us as if we were their sons, crying with joy. My God, what they must have been through to greet us in that way? As the women continued in their excitement about meeting us, we tried to swallow our meal. In fact, we devoured it, regardless of any courtesy. We could not do otherwise after all we had been through.

During the meal, a lovely lady, Mrs Arndt, burst into the house. You could see that she was clearly very happy. She had brought a dozen eggs in her apron and after cutting off a piece of lard, threw it into a pan and cracked the eggs in with it. Her hands were shaking with joyful excitement and in her zeal, two of the eggs she broke missed the pan. We were to eat and eat. We certainly did not need any encouragement to do so. We were still hungry, even though each of us was given half a loaf of well-baked bread. The women enjoyed watching us eat. They were happy to help us.

The mystery of the pigs was also solved: the women were going to kill one of them that morning. They told us about their horrible experiences when the Russians had passed that way over the last few weeks, and they had to run into the woods every time. We knew our enemy's habits after fighting him in the East, and the three years we had spent there had allowed us to know the 'culture' they now wished to instil in us Germans. Despite, this, we still listened to women's stories with horror.

Waldemar was assigned to slaughter the pigs. Our nutritional situation was thus improving dramatically. We also learned that the people there still had 150 kilos of rye flour. More civilians gradually emerged from the forest, and we eventually counted eighteen people who had been hiding from the hordes of Russians in the darkness of the forest. We would soon meet them all and become acquainted with one another. They all came from the town of Człopy, 15 kilometres away, and were the families and close friends of the local residents. Throughout the day, we alternated between sleeping and eating – the women could not get over how much food we consumed! There was a blizzard outside and we had no winter or camouflage clothing. With the women's permission, we decided to stay in the house for some time.

Three days into our stay, we came up with the idea that after three weeks of wandering, we should finally wash and shave properly. We were so dishevelled we hardly recognized each other anymore. Our situation had changed dramatically and we knew we owed our lives to the existence of those people who had welcomed us so graciously.

The inhabitants of Człopy, to whom the author and his companions owed their lives.

A Respite

The incessant blizzard and our poor health made us ask our hostesses if we could stay with them for a while. Some members of this large family were against the idea, but the women, who clearly had the deciding vote, agreed that we should rest before venturing out into the unknown again. For those who had survived the encounters with the Russians, the presence of our weapons was certainly handy, but we also knew that the Russians had put death notices up in the towns for those found to be hosting or helping German soldiers. This was certainly not conducive to our hosts' sense of security. Meanwhile, an element of understanding was slowly being established between us that in the event of an attack, they would follow us into the fire.

It was now 12 March, and together with my comrades-in-arms, we were busy baking potatoes when two civilians on bicycles showed up unexpectedly in the yard. It turned out that they were members of the Volkssturm who were breaking through to the neighbouring village. With horror in their eyes, they told us about a third member of their group who had been blown to smithereens in a nearby minefield. After listening to their detailed report, it became clear to us that we had also passed that way a few days earlier. Even two of our new friends had been there just the day before looking for fuel. We looked at each other and unanimously concluded that a special guardian angel must have been watching over us. In the afternoon, the two men moved on, hoping to get back to their families as soon as possible.

The next morning, one of the men returned to tell us that his companion had been arrested by the Russians but that he had managed to escape. He wanted to stay with us and although we were not keen on the idea, we could not refuse him. There were more and more of us, and our group now consisted of twenty-four people, which forced our hosts to kill the second pig. During the day the women hid in the farm buildings, while the elderly stayed in a forester's lodge and we lived in the large house, having arranged some hay in the attic for somewhere to sleep. It was not particularly comfortable, especially now that there was one more of us, and because we were unable to come downstairs during the day.

In the evenings we would meet up in the forester's lodge and talk about our homeland and about what we had been through. Our hosts, as they say, had not only lost their patrimony and possessions, but also their faith in a better tomorrow. We tried to lift their spirits, especially because it helped to make us feel better. Gradually, we managed to make smiles rather than tears appear on their faces. The two women to whom we owed the most, and whose names I would like to mention now, were the unforgettable Mrs Arndt and her sister, Mrs Wellnitz. They fought for their right to live every day, sneaking into nearby houses and searching them meticulously. With great caution and determination they tried to dig out anything salvageable from the rubble that might have been useful on the farm. They could quickly assess the situation and retreat, when necessary, thereby resembling real soldiers in their actions.

It was nearly 21 March: the birthday of our two companions. Resigning caution, we left our hideouts and sat down at a table covered with a white cloth in front of the forester's lodge. There was even cake after an exquisite dinner. Waldemar had a particular sense of humour and suggested that for fun, we should express our birthday wishes by impersonating the honorary members from Człopa. He was a pastor, Horst pretended to be a representative of the Frauenshaft [Women's League], Kurt was a village teacher, and I was a civil servant. Tears of joy flowed down our faces that day.

Above and below: The birthday party in Rohrfort showing the festive table in front of the forester's lodge. Hanitzsch and Horst are on the left. Waldemar is on the right.

Our meat supply was running low and so following the advice of a civilian, in the afternoon of 29 March we went out to fetch some pigs from a farm 25 kilometres away. The aforementioned man guided us with a sense of complete security, especially as we were armed. After walking for about 5 kilometres, past the demolished Płociczno [Plotzenfliess] forester's lodge[58] we crossed a large road. Alongside were the fortifications of the southern section of the Pomeranian Wall. We saw a Russian on guard in one of the concrete bunkers. Next to him, in a large meadow, a beautiful cow was grazing peacefully. We decided to take it. The three of us took up positions facing the bunker, our weapons ready to fire in case the guard noticed us. In the meantime, Waldemar and the civilian put a halter on the cow and quickly drove it towards the forest. We led the animal back to the forester's lodge, arousing general admiration from the residents. However, the whole operation had been decidedly risky.

The next day, Waldemar and I decided to kill the cow. The women expressed their disbelief, doubting we would be able to handle such a large animal. An hour and a half later, however, we had proved to them that we had not forgotten what we had learned in Russia. We carried the heavy pieces of meat into the forest, which soon began to look like a butcher's shop. Once again, we now had plenty of food and did not have to be afraid of hunger. In the meantime, we discovered a huge mound of potatoes, which we reckoned must have weighed about 5 tonnes. Both the aforementioned women took on the role of cooks, assisted by their daughters, while we were tasked with bringing water and fuel.

Easter was coming and it was time to start preparing for the festivities. The surviving hens lay so many eggs that each of us had two almost every day. On Easter Saturday we even tried to paint them as a present for the children. The first day of the holiday, however, did not begin so carefree. At 07.00 we found out that we would have to shoot someone. A man from a nearby village, who had sold himself to the Russians, came in his covered wagon to steal our chickens. The women resisted him, but he threatened to return with the Cossacks. In response, Mrs Arndt grabbed a wooden stake and struck the traitor with it. When he realized we were going to have to kill him, he ran away in a panic. He must have whipped his horse hard because he soon disappeared and by the time we got to the road, he was gone.

We returned to the farm and posted guards to greet the Cossacks with dignity, but no one appeared that Easter weekend. We admired Mrs Arndt for her courage and strength. Meanwhile, our meat supply was running out again and for two days we had nothing but watery soup for dinner. We were sat at the table when our boys reported that a few domestic animals were wandering in the woods, so we set out on a search and found four sheep and two goats. We herded them into the yard and locked them in the stable. These were big prey. We killed them and thanked God for having something to eat again. Two days later, we even found a grazing cow, while another was brought by a resident of Marthe (Martew). The well-fed animals gave us a several litres of milk every day. You could say we lived quite well there.

However, on the afternoon of 12 April, the situation changed. A group of six heavily armed Poles emerged from the forest on bicycles. They were deserters and had caused great confusion in the area. Luckily, we were not home at the time. The visitors told the women that there were seventeen more soldiers waiting for them by the road. They ate their fill, took the ham and lard, and disappeared. Later that evening they returned unexpectedly, but thank God one of those brave women had warned us in time. In the morning, Waldemar and I went out to the edge of the forest and watched the Poles wandering around the farmyard from a distance. They were still sitting there, which meant we had to look for an alternative shelter. Mrs Arndt led us to Salmer-Teerofen [the Hermitage], where there was a small wooden hut near the forest, previously used by the men who had built the Pomeranian Wall. We dismantled the building and, piece by piece, laboriously moved it several hundred metres into the forest to rebuild it there.

We worked from dawn to dusk, paying particular attention to making it camouflaged. As the elders and the women with the children had stayed behind at the forester's lodge, there were now sixteen of us in our new shelter. We gradually brought the meat and in a cellar in the burnt-out village of Miradz [Grüneberg], we found several hundred kilos of rye. We next looked for coffee grinders so that each of us could grind a certain amount of rye. We took the unleavened bread to a previous forester's lodge, Rogoźnica [Räumde], where we baked the bread under the cover of night. We were in particular danger when carrying the water and potatoes, because we had to cross the road each time.

We came across many dead as we scouted around the lodge, including a large number of dead Russians. We consequently got to know our surroundings very well and knew that we were in a forest square with a side about 1 kilometre long, surrounded on all sides by roads. One of them was frequently used by Russian units and we often heard shouts in enemy language, sometimes accompanied by shots. It was most intense in the afternoon so when silence fell in the evening, we all breathed a sigh of relief. One night, we had returned to Rogoźnica to bake more bread when Waldemar said: 'I hope the Russians won't come here.' He had an odd feeling.

The next day, 24 April, Waldemar and I slept until 09.00. As we went outside to wash, we heard the sound of Russian engines in the distance again. We also heard gunfire. The women picked up the potato peelings to boil them, while we intuitively packed up and grabbed our weapons. We were not yet fully dressed when the enemy appeared in front of the hut. They must have sneaked up there silently, and immediately began to open fire with their submachine guns. We all scattered in a panic. At the last moment, I grabbed my coat and some bread before falling to the ground. We ran away into the forest, but there were eight, maybe ten, Russians running behind us, shooting wildly. I was being chased by a squat Mongol. When he was about twenty paces from me, his gun jammed. The bolt obviously did not close, and I heard him pull the trigger idly. As a result, he did not fire at Hanitzsch, who was running about 5 metres in front of him, who, in his nervousness, had not even pulled out his own pistol.

Meanwhile, the Russians had emptied their first magazines, meaning we had a small advantage. Yet they continued their pursuit. When we were finally beyond their firing range, we saw the women running towards us and together we reached the young forest next to the Rogoźnica forester's lodge. We sought temporary accommodation there and asked for help from a family living nearby. Gradually, more and more victims of 'the hunt' came to us. By evening, only two 18-year-olds and Mrs Schuman were missing. Mrs Arndt arrived later with little 8-year-old Horst. She was carrying a heavy backpack. Finally, both boys showed up. One of them, Hervard Schuman, had been attacked by the Russians. His mother had collapsed in front of the hut; heart disease having taken away her strength to escape. Her son had been kneeling down beside her when the returning Russians had caught him and dragged him inside. They then proceeded to beat him on the back and head with their rifle butts until he started to bleed from his nose. He managed to escape by taking advantage of a lapse in their concentration. Thank God the bullets fired after him did not reach him.

We returned to our hut at night with our weapons. The Russians were no longer there but had still smashed everything to pieces. They had also taken anything they regarded as valuable, including the women's abandoned backpacks and a goat tied in front of the hut. All the dishes and cutlery were scattered around.

We looked around for anything useful and, when we were about to leave, discovered the body of the dead Mrs Schuman, laying right in the place her son had described. Her skull was shattered and a small pouch containing all her personal belongings (10,000 marks and a wedding ring) had been ripped from her neck. We stood shocked by the corpse of a defenceless woman who had fallen victim to the Russian assault. We felt most sorry for her son, who was now alone after his father had left with the Volkssturm troops long before. Feeling helpless and depressed, we hid the next day in a grove near Sitnica [Marienthal]. The Russians searched the area around our hut for several hours, firing and throwing hand grenades blindly, as if they wanted to kill every mouse in the forest.

A day later, Horst set off on a scouting mission and upon his return told us that there was a hunting lodge a few kilometres away and that, surprisingly, German soldiers were living there following an unsuccessful attempt to break through the front on the Oder. Their Hauptmann (who in civilian life was a forester from East Prussia) had remembered the lodge from his time training in the area. There were two Leutnants and an Obergefreiter with him, and now that we had comrades in misery nearby, we did not feel so alone.

On the evening of 28 April we set off to visit our old quarters in Rohfort again. No one else had been there since the arrival of the Polish deserters. Shortly after our arrival, the elderly people who had been living there decided to move back to their hometown of Człopy. It was a beautiful time for us. Once again, we had two cows, three sheep and six chickens. We also had potatoes. Furthermore, the Hauptmann promised to teach us how to hunt deer. However, it was not him, but Horst who managed to shoot a deer after a few days, after which we ate our first roast of venison. The Hauptmann lent us some rye flour from his stocks and so we had fresh bread every week. I took over as baker and every Tuesday morning would bake sixteen large loaves.

Meanwhile, our calendar showed that it was 12 May. We were all living very well and felt in excellent health, but that goddam uncertainty remained. Almost every day we grabbed our guns as soon as we heard shots coming from a distance. Since the Russians' last visit, we had been carrying our weapons with us constantly, jumping up nervously at each shot and taking position in the windows.

One day, we found some leaflets in the forest. We read about the fighting near Kassel and in the Ruhr area.[59] Every sentence was a blow for us, but we told ourselves it could not be entirely true, and that it was a piece of misleading propaganda information. We could hear the distant thunder of artillery from the other side of the Oder and believed that the front would reach us soon.

Our civilian friend, who snuck out every night to his house in Sitnica for news, told us that the war had ended three days earlier. We laughed at him, saying that if it were true, bells would have rung out in nearby towns on 9 May to announce the end of the war. By noon, we had convinced him enough that he had started to doubt it himself, and on the afternoon of the same day, Mrs Arndt and Mrs Jacobi went to Człopy to visit their grandparents and inquire. Gefreiter Frohlich, who had joined us in the meantime, accompanied them. In the evening, the officer returned alone. It appeared that the women had been arrested by the Poles and were unable to leave town. We were very worried about them.

The next day greeted us with sunshine. It was 13 May and Waldemar's twenty-fifth birthday. Once again, however, we had to hide from cars passing nearby. It turned out that we had a great sniper among us: Uncle Ernst would go hunting everyday with his silver 'Winnetou rifle' and almost every time brought back new prey. Our meat supplies were in no danger of running out. During the day we lay in the sun and read. One of us had the idea of digging a fallow field and planting potatoes. We did not know who would end up picking them, but at least we had some useful occupation in that wilderness. We worked in the field and that is how time passed by.

We were in constant contact with the Hauptmann and his group, and one evening we decided to go and visit them in the hunting lodge. We could only undertake such actions at night because we had to cross the roads. Besides, the Russians were also hunting in the surrounding forests. That day, Waldemar and I saw the Hauptmann for the first time and were pleasantly surprised by the officer's elegance. He was a battalion commander and had won many military awards. As a forest inspector, he had often met with officers from noble Prussian families, and he told us about his experiences serving in the Pomeranian Regiment. When we met him, he had changed his uniform to that of the forest inspector and looked very impressive in it, with a lush but well-kept stubble. His principled and disciplined manner helped us to trust him implicitly, and we imagined him as the commander of the 'Thal' Battle Group we had jointly created. Later, we invited him and his group to visit us at Pentecost. He duly promised to come in a couple of days, and we began to prepare for his visit.

We decorated our lodge with red and white lilac and placed young birches in front of the entrance. We even put up welcome signs and the name of our hut (Villa Reizenstein).[60] We cooked and baked as if it were peacetime. We prepared beds in a nearby grove, next to a small bunker, and solemnly welcomed our guests the day before the holidays. The moment was so sublime it is almost impossible to describe. The first day of the holidays was Mother's Day, and one of the women who was still with us (the unforgettable Mrs Wellnitz) was very excited about it. We brought the most beautiful and rarest flowers from the gardens of the ravaged neighbouring town, and each of us gave her a bouquet. She was so touched by the celebration of this day, prepared by her 'war children', that tears ran down her face.

After breakfast, we showed our guests around. The Hauptmann was absolutely delighted with our accommodation and its surroundings. Dinner had its own special setting. We took our seats at a log table covered with a white tablecloth. Our distinguished guest sat at one end, Mrs Wellnitz at the other. Each chair was decorated with red or white lilac, and even the table had been decorated by our girls. The hostesses gracefully served festive food to everyone. The sun shone brightly in the sky, a light wind played softly with the birch trees, and the sweet, intense scent of flowers floated in the air. We felt like screaming with joy. After dinner, some people rested in a forest clearing, while others took a boat trip on the stream. On the first day of the holiday, no shots were fired, and we could enjoy the peace.

Our guests stayed with us for a few more days before we all parted with heavy hearts. We had celebrated this time like nowhere else in a country occupied by the enemy. Those unique and splendid days will certainly remain in our memory for a long time.

In the meantime, the first refugees from northern Germany arrived. We now heard the news from their lips that the war was really over and that the German state was completely occupied by hostile forces. We could not understand it. After all, we could still hear shooting, and the thunder of the guns in the west did not cease. We could not believe that the Russians were the victors of this war. Our Hauptmann said that the struggle between the victorious forces would not end, declaring that he would be the first to be placed at the disposal of the Western Bloc whenever a conflict arose. But at that time, at least, it seemed that moment would not come anytime soon.

Close to the village of Moczele [Marzelle], the Hauptmann showed us his shooting skills during an unexpected meeting with the Poles. The commander, with his two Leutnants, lay at the edge of the forest and watched the troop operations happening nearby. Suddenly, two armed Poles began heading towards the tree line, and all three of them immediately stood ready to fire. The Hauptman let the enemy approach to a distance of 300 metres. He aimed at one himself and left the second to his soldiers. He shot first, aiming for the head.[61] The Pole threw his arms in the air and fell on his face. Shots were then fired at the other man, but he managed to escape and hide behind the village buildings. The captain's small unit had built a few spacious bunkers near the hunting lodge, providing the residents of the nearest town of Zatom [Zatten] the opportunity to hide their belongings and, if necessary, also themselves. In gratitude, they gave the soldiers large amounts of flour.

One day, a Russian deserter appeared in the town and began to cause serious trouble for the residents. He harassed the women and ordered them to prepare the most exquisite meals for himself. He found quarters on the first floor of a two-storey family house and ordered the hosts' daughter to serve him. Her father told us that the Hauptmann had decided to get rid of the Russian. At first, the civilian refused, but he finally agreed to help. They agreed that they would proceed the following evening, when the old man was to hang a white flag on the roof to show that the Leutnant was at home. When the signal appeared, the Hauptmann and his escort stepped inside and tried to operate as efficiently as possible. The old man (whose real name was Köpp, although everyone called him Grandpa) let him know that his daughter was also upstairs. The Hauptmann and his two companions cautiously ascended the stairs, and soon all that was left of the Russian was an old colt, two watches and an uneaten delicious supper of grilled fish prepared by the host's daughter.[62]

On 28 May, the Hauptmann and his unit came to us at Rohrfort. He told us that armed Polish militiamen (in plain clothes) had ridden to his quarters on bikes and opened up a deadly fire on them. However, the Hauptman and his people had managed to break out of the trap laid by the enemy. From that moment on, they would stay with us and we would lead the fight against adversity together.

The Hauptmann introduced us to the secrets of hunting. So far, only our Uncle Ernst had any merit when it came to hunting. Whenever we were short of food, he would go out to shoot a big deer. Now, however, each of us discovered our own hunting abilities, and we would go out alone or with the Hauptmann and Uncle Ernst. With time, we became very keen hunters and would get up before dawn to look for game in the forest, whose wilderness we had come to regard as our saviour. We took the opportunity to get to know the forest animals and admire their habits. All the wonders of this 'rich and blessed nature' were revealed to us. We often lay at the edge of a forest clearing by Lake Sitno and watched as huge herds of deer came down to the watering hole at dawn. It was wonderful to be able to observe those majestic animals with their huge antlers. Our hearts pounded like a hammer when one with eight or ten prongs passed us by. We never saw one with twelve. We shivered when we heard the roar of a deer in the dark of the evening. Those sounds seemed human-like to me.

A walk along the lake shore in those first hours of the day had a unique charm. You have to have your eyes and ears open to recognize the mating sounds of waterbirds. As soon as the sun came up, stately swans would appear on the lake. We were surprised that nature could restore peace and tranquillity so quickly after being disturbed by men and war.

One evening, Waldemar and I spent over an hour sitting on the hunting platform to hunt deer from up there. However, we lacked the patience experienced hunters have, so we climbed down and set off to sneak up on a herd of deer that were calmly walking across the meadow in front of us. Unfortunately, the animals picked up our scent and ran away, and chasing after them was pointless. In the evening, the Hauptmann explained to us why it is so difficult to sneak up on deer. Meanwhile, it turned out we had been extra unlucky. Near the hunting platform where we had been sitting only an hour before, a huge herd of deer had passed by on their way to the watering hole. Scared by our attention, they had run away and passed us by about 20 metres before disappearing into the forest that protected them. Our two shots fired at the largest individuals had missed their target, and the experience clearly showed us how much patience was needed when hunting.

One evening, we went hunting with the Hauptmann. We had noticed a goat eating quietly by our forester's lodge, and using binoculars had worked out that it was an adult male. The Hauptmann wanted to shoot it at once, even though we were 200 or 250 metres away. He was so confident that he rested his weapon against his boot for a moment and, as we shook our heads in disbelief, said: 'Please, observe through the binoculars.' He took aim and fired. When he asked me what I had seen, I told him I was sorry to say I had not seen the animal fall. He smiled and told me that he had not missed. Looking at the movements of the wounded animal, he could judge where it had been hit. The 'Hunter's Greeting' rang out cheerfully and on the way to the stream, the Hauptmann explained that the goat's dancing walk indicated that it had been shot in the liver. He gutted the billy goat very professionally (in four minutes) and I could see for myself where the animal had been wounded. We failed to find any wild boars, although the Hauptmann had supposedly shot one at his previous headquarters.

Uncle Ernst came for dinner one evening. When we heard a shot fired at about 21.30 (usually always at the same time), one of us would stand up and say: 'God help him'. We meant, of course, the deer shot by the 'Winnetou rifle'. Only once did Uncle Ernst miss, and the fact that he only fired when he was sure of success proved he was an excellent hunter.

Bringing our prey home was always the hardest part. After all, each deer weighed several kilos. When one evening we managed to shoot three deer, transporting them back to our lodge through the forest took us until midnight. In this way, however, our stocks never ran out. According to tradition, the hunter must eat the brain of the hunted animal himself, and the women would prepare it in a sophisticated way. We would have a leg for breakfast, a roast with potatoes for lunch and a roast again for dinner. During our stay in Rohrfort, we killed a total of eighteen roe deer and twelve deer.

Once, my attention was caught by an arctic fox with a fabulous fur tail, and I wondered if he might be a target for me too. It had escaped from a nearby, dilapidated farm in Friedland[63] and had been wandering around our neighbourhood half-feral. I had tried to sneak up on it for days, but it was always alert and would run away from me. Once we even met a pack of hunting dogs. I had never seen anything like them before. The animals rushed through the forest crazily, at great speed, and it was not difficult to imagine that the other wild animals of the forest would have little chance of escaping from such attackers.

It would soon be 8 June. Summer had arrived in Rohrfort and for me the holidays of 1945 had just begun. If anyone from the outside world was watching us, they would not have believed that we were in hiding. Our friendly civilian had acquired a lot of courage and flair during his forest life, and, along with the Gefreiter, under the cover of a misty night stole a pig from the new mayor (a Pole) of his hometown. The pig weighed 36 kilos after killing. On another day they boldly stole bicycles from recently arrived Poles and would later be a hair's breadth from a heroic death after their original owners followed the tyre tracks.

Seven German soldiers who had been released from captivity in Gdańsk stopped in a nearby village. They were heading west, but after meeting us were captured again by the Russians. Our enemies scoured the local forests hoping to meet more of our compatriots. We stayed alert throughout the day and even built a defensive 'hedgehog' around the farmyard. The Hauptmann gave us orders through a liaison, and we took up positions in the appropriate places. The women crossed the stream and hid deep inside the forest. Meanwhile, we were at the highest combat readiness. We heard bullets whistling through the pines, but the Russians passed about a kilometre away without noticing our lodge. We thanked God for that.

A few days later, we paid a visit to a family living in a forest lodge about 8 kilometres away.[64] The hosts' daughters worked in the fields, and there was a railway embankment nearby leading to Wałcz. We learned that enemy troops and tanks were being transported that way to the East, thus proving that the war had ended. We could only hope that the new borders were not yet fully closed. The events of the next few days convinced us once and for all that the hostilities were over, when we saw Russian troops marching continuously along the main road from Miradz to Człopy, about 3 kilometres from our base. It had been going on since 11 June. At night, we heard the roar of animals and realized that the Russians were driving herds of cows to the East. We also heard insults and curses, while shots were fired every other moment. Later, we heard the rattle of cars covered with tarpaulins. We sent two young scouts up towards the road, where they could finally see for themselves that enemy regiments were marching east. Vehicles laden with weapons and equipment passed one after the other and were followed by infantry soldiers, singing and shouting. Armed female units were marching by, too.

We received a message from the loyal people of Człopy, who would come to us from time to time, that troops were continuing to move east. Their town had also seen several transports of prisoners pass through. A family from Neumuhl[65] told us that entire armoured units were rolling along the railway. We were slowly beginning to accept the thought that we would soon need to start breaking through in the opposite direction. We knew it was a long way off, but we tried to prepare ourselves for it. The girls and two boys found it difficult to get used to the idea that when we left, they would have to go to Człopy to serve the Russians. The local Germans were meanwhile being tormented by the new mayor and the militia. Woe to those who did not comply with their demands. One commandant ordered you to pick berries, another demanded you mow the grass with kitchen knives. All agricultural equipment and tools were packed up and shipped deep into Russia. The remaining men were forced to load the rest of their belongings onto wagons. Everything made of steel and iron had to be dismantled and made ready for the road, just like everything else the Russians found useful.

The Hauptmann wanted to leave with his group a week before us, so we prepared provisions for them to keep them safe on the road. In the early evening of 30 June, they said goodbye to us, full of faith that they would achieve their set goal. We spent the following days carefully hiding all the goods we had. We hid the household appliances, flour, and rye so that the women who stayed there could come back from Człopy for them if they were hungry. Next, we tried to prepare ourselves for the road. In addition to bread, the women packed us some pre-prepared specialties. Mrs Arndt made us three beautifully cured sausages from deer meat and pork fat, hanging them in the smokehouse for several days. We also took a supply of beetroot syrup and lard so as not to get hungry.

The women living in Człopa did everything they could to look after their companions of misfortune who lived nearby, and when 6 July arrived, we began to say our goodbyes. It was very hard to part with Mrs Wellnitz and her family. Mrs Arndt also slipped out of town to wish us all the best for the future. We were unable to repay them with similar wishes, knowing that we were abandoning them to their own fate in their hometown. The moment of farewell was just as touching as the one when we had first met. Now there was silence in Rohrfort. Even our civilian was quiet, even though not so long before he had been screaming terribly after we had killed a sheep before our journey. We would miss the loud laughter and uproar. We walked around in circles, delaying the final moment of departure. We even took the remaining china and cutlery to our forest shelters, and later wrote heartfelt farewell letters. It was now 7 July, and we knew we would have to leave the following day. None of us could sleep that night.

The Road to Freedom

'On that fateful day, 8 July 1945, four German officers laid down their arms, changed from their uniforms to civilian clothes, and set off on a historic journey.' These words by our wonderful colleague from Dresden, Hanitzsch, were the prologue of our march to freedom. It was 16.00 when we put our heavy backpacks on our shoulders to follow the path we had carefully marked out, after studying maps for hours. We had marked every bit of forest, every village we would have to go around, every road we would have to cross, calculating all the distances precisely. We set off hoping to reach a large forest complex near Breń [Bernsee] the next day.

At first we followed the paths we knew and then crossed the main Miradz – Załom – Człopy road. After a while we passed the ruins of the Rogoźnica forester's lodge and looked back once more towards the grove where we had hidden. We went through the area around Sitnica before reaching Moczele. We sometimes had to hide from the Russians and Poles who were passing that way, but eventually we reached the bridge over the Drawa. We looked carefully left and right and then ran over it quickly. We arched around a village and headed west along a path that led through a wonderful deciduous forest. It was pleasing to our eyes as we had only seen pine and spruce forests for the previous six months. After dusk we deviated a little from the road. On the right was the village of Radachowo [Heidekavel], which was well-known to our friend, Sandrock, following his first attempt to break through to the frontline.

We knocked on the door of the first house. The frightened residents did not want to open it, but after a while we saw a man's face appear in the window. After a brief consultation with the women, the man invited us inside and introduced himself as Leutnant von Firo. He had been taken prisoner near Królewiec [Konigsberg] and then jumped out of the railway carriage transporting him to Siberia. He had made his way from East Prussia and had decided to stay a little longer in Radachowo to rest before continuing his march west (he was a manufacturer in Leipzig). He had told the authorities there he was a bursar and was registered as such at the Russian headquarters. His plan was to stay until the political situation had stabilized a bit. We were warmly welcomed and because our friend was sick, we also decided to stay a little longer.

For two weeks we went hunting every evening and thus supplied the local residents with meat. We were all doing quite well. One Sunday we even risked hunting during the day, taking care not to run into any Poles and Russians who were doing the same. There were three other German soldiers in a neighbouring village. One of them (a law student from western Germany) had pretended to be 'mad' in front the Russians and had been hiding his true identity for several months, making sure his gestures and speech resembled the behaviour of a mentally ill person. He did all this so he would not have to work as hard, which was how he ended up grazing cows. He could not fail to hide his satisfaction. However, he brought us fresh milk every day and I admire people with such a theatrical talent.

Every German soldier could now obtain demobilization documents, so on the evening of 23 July, we set off once more. The interviews we had carried out in the meantime about the Oder line had not proved satisfactory, but we wanted to see it for ourselves. In the evening we crossed the main road from Gorzów Wielkopolski to Kostrzyn,[66]which in the coming days would be crossed by thousands of freed soldiers. For a moment we considered the idea of joining a column of prisoners, but quickly came to the conclusion that we would achieve our goal faster if we went separately. On the left we passed several larger towns occupied by the Russians, and when the sun rose among the mist, we lay down to rest in a small grove.

We planned the next stages of our journey that afternoon, then set off in the evening. We passed through a large forest complex located on the eastern shore of the Oder,[67] and after following the forest paths, the next morning reached a forester's lodge by a large lake.[68] It really was beautiful there. The rooms inside the house looked the same as all others we had seen before. We filled our canteens at the pump and went to sleep in a tent we pitched nearby. Despite the gradual depletion of our food, our bodies were now in much better condition and the hardships of the journey did not tire us as much. We were about to move on when we saw a Russian sitting on the pier. He also spotted us and watched us carefully. In order to avoid him, we went around the forester's lodge in a giant arc, and soon found ourselves making our way through gorges, impenetrable forest thickets, and pine forests. The Russians had many ammunition depots in those areas, so we carefully walked around all the fenced outposts, often having to retreat whenever we heard human voices and dogs barking.

We spent the next day near a large lake, and when we moved on, we suddenly had to hide from two men on bicycles. When we met German residents later in the evening, we found out that they were a Polish woodsman and a German who was working for him. Having received this important information, we marched on and reached Gajewo [Nesselgrund][69] in the morning of 26 July. Some of the houses there were empty, but soon two women from Bochum opened a door. We talked over bread and coffee. They admired us and hoped we would be able to return to our homeland. They directed us to an isolated farm nearby, where a German woman from the Volga region lived. She offered us an attic and we spent the whole day there. In the morning, we were able to observe the Russians from our hiding place as they repeatedly passed through the yard. There were about a dozen of them, and during breaks from work would often sit by the pump for a drink of water. Our attention was particularly drawn to the figure of a Russian lieutenant, who brought our hostesses a bale of German fabric and ordered them to sew a stylish uniform from it. We could see him very clearly because he was standing only 20 metres from us, leaning against his vehicle. So, this was the representative of the current, new government? He did not look very dignified for a Soviet officer.

Meanwhile, the news of our stay was spreading around the village. An old lady came to visit us first. She gave us meat and bread, then, with tears in her eyes, begged us to abandon our plans. She spoke with horror about the terrible barbed wire and minefields on the banks of the Oder. In the evening, a positive pilgrimage of residents came to our accommodation. We noticed with a smile that the women and girls had dressed up to meet us, and even brought gifts! In addition to cold cuts and bread, we received other foodstuffs and were able to eat well. Our hostess suggested we report to the local commander's translator (a Ukrainian lady). As she spoke two languages fluently – German and Russian – she could therefore help us with our demobilization cards.

The woman in question appeared the next evening. Our friend Sandrock from Nuremberg acted as our representative and conducted the negotiations, persuading the Ukrainian woman to issue the appropriate papers for the five of us. The woman trembled with fear as she forged the war commissioner's and doctor's signatures on each document. We swore our absolute discretion and bid her a happy farewell, before conferring with each other when best to move on. I was the only one who wanted to go during the day and although I did not feel very confident about it, I figured it was time to lay all our cards on the table again to achieve our goal. After a slight hesitation, the others agreed with me. None of us slept that night. We all felt too anxious, knowing that what we intended to do would require the greatest courage so far. We had been marching, fighting and surviving in the darkness for months, and now we were going to expose ourselves, moving among the Russians and trying to talk to the Poles. I must admit I was tormented by similar feelings to those I had in Russia: fear of the future and the uncertainty of fate.

It was 06.00 on 28 July. After walking along a drainage ditch, we reached a road and strode along it, boldly. We knew at any moment we might meet a Russian who would pull out a gun and ask what we were doing there. After a while, a huge mill standing on the riverbank emerged on the horizon. In the square in front of this three-storey building, two Polish soldiers were stood next to a car. We tried to control our emotions as Jochen approached them, tilting his hat and stretching out his hand towards them in a gesture of greeting. We realized this was our first important meeting with our 'new neighbours'. The Pole did not ask us to show any documents, but instead eagerly provided us with information about the right way we needed to travel. We moved on and soon heard submachine gun fire from behind us. We turned around, convinced that we were being hunted, but it was not about us this time.

Near the road to Kostrzyn, which we had to cross, were the remains of an abandoned stalag, and we could see evidence of fierce struggles that had taken place there. In front of us lay the town of Mosina [Massin],[70] near Gorzów, and the town of Witnica nearby. We asked a German girl standing in the field, cheerfully talking to a young Pole, for directions, but received no clear information from her. Instead, we rested in a village barn and asked about the situation for the Germans working nearby. Meanwhile, Jochen approached a Russian commander who drove to Berlin every day with a transport of potatoes. We wanted to find out if it was possible to hitch a ride on one of the trucks. After a while, Jochen returned with the commander, who was a sergeant, and his French assistant. We showed them our documents and were then escorted to their headquarters where we met another Russian, who ordered us to hand over all our belongings.

Shortly thereafter, we were locked in a dark cellar with barred windows. The only thing we were given was some bread and water and a handful of straw for bedding. We were devastated and could not believe our fate. Women and girls from the village appeared at the cellar window. They brought us food and we gave them our maps and notes. I could not swallow a mouthful, and when we found out what awaited us, chills ran down our spines. The women said that if the Russians discovered who we really were, we would be shot immediately. If not, we would be flogged instead. We were to be interrogated by an officer from Witnica, which was not good news. We sat there in that torture cell in the local commandant's office, with nothing but bread and water, waiting for what fate would bring us. The minutes dragged on like hours. We were depressed in soul and body. From time to time, a single ray of sunshine fell through into our dark cellar. We had become prisoners of the Soviet Army.

We slowly realized that our attempt to cross the new border had ended in failure, and the situation we had found ourselves in was serious. After two hours, we heard the clank of bolts on the prison door. It was time for our interrogation. A lieutenant, a translator and two other Russians entered the cell, accompanied by the sergeant armed with a large truncheon. We leapt to our feet, but the officer immediately ordered us to sit down. We anxiously awaited further developments. The sergeant thrust the truncheon forwards, and I tensed my muscles in anticipation of the blow. But he only asked – as a kind of joke – if it was our property, and when we denied it, he put it aside with a sneer. Then the officer, with the help of the translator, started the interrogation. He asked each of us in turn, starting with me, and I referred to him my completely new, made-up CV. I told him that I had never been in the army, and that at the age of 19 I was serving on the railway in Piła as a telephone operator. I had been arrested by the Russians and placed in a camp near Skórka, but due to illness I was released with my friends on 25 June.

My other comrades said the same. The officer also wanted to know whether we had had any weaponry training. We denied it again. He asked a few more general questions, to which he received quick and decisive answers. To our astonishment, he pulled our demobilization cards out of his pocket, smoothed them down on his thigh and, after reading out the names, gave us the documents. Although we wanted to visit the houses of the women who had helped us to collect our maps and notes, the officer ordered us to leave town within ten minutes. We dreamed of nothing else and so, breathing a sigh of relief, set off on the road to Kostrzyn. An hour earlier our hearts had been pounding like hammers, but now we were laughing again and enjoying our freedom. We asked Jochen if he knew why we were arrested. He told us that the Russians had not noticed that our documents were forged, but the Frenchman had noticed the lack of a stamp.

From asking people along the way, we found out that the best place to cross the Oder was in Kostrzyn, rather than looking for a crossing beyond the mouth of the Warta. We left the road and crossed the moors, reaching the A1 (Reichsstasse 1) motorway running south, which we needed to get to Berlin. As a group of five, we realized that we were drawing more and more attention to ourselves, and so decided to split up. This was a very difficult decision for us, even though we knew perfectly well it was absolutely necessary because we had to pass through two villages where Russian and Polish troops were stationed. We decided that the three of us from the south would go first, then Waldemar and I would follow after a short interval. It was difficult to part from the companions with whom we had shared all our joys and sorrows.

Following in our friends' footsteps, we reached the main road. Every now and then we were stopped by Russians and Poles asking us where we were going. Just before Kostrzyn, we had to pass a building where Polish artillerymen were stationed. The guard stood at the booth also checked us out. At about 21.00 we reached the ruins of Kostrzyn and stopped for the night in the suburbs. We spread out on the floor of a former rabbit hutch or chicken coop. We heard shots coming from the city. We knew we were very close to the bridge over the Oder, and it was this awareness that kept us awake.

In the cool morning of Sunday, 29 July, with a light rain falling, we left our shelter and began our approach to the bridge. As we passed through the city centre, it was hard to find a surviving house. There must have been fierce fighting there. At every intersection the Russians had placed tall victory columns painted red, covered with posters and decorated with a big star on the top. They looked very oriental. We looked at all the huge portraits of Stalin and the commanders of the liberating army with disapproval and disgust. As we approached the first bridge over a branch of the Oder, we showed our documents to the Polish guard and walked to the other side. After a few hundred metres we met a column of Russian soldiers going west. We joined them and crossed the second bridge – the bigger one, over the Oder proper – together.

The Russians looked at us warily, but only asked if we had any cigarettes. In the middle of the bridge, the guards checked our documents again and were surprised they were all written in the same way. When we reached the other side, we thanked Providence for looking after us. We kept repeating to ourselves: 'It's a pity our loved ones can't see us now.'

Unfortunately, further progress along the main road became impossible after some women from the traffic regulation company told us to leave it, indicating an alternative direction with a gun and a signal flag. We were now marching northwest on a side road towards Wriezen. We passed prisoners of war who had been released from Gorzów Wielkopolski, consisting of young anti-aircraft gunners and a few old, infirm men. We looked on at the remains of the once proud Wehrmacht with great pain.

We tried to walk fast, aiming to cover a distance of 40-50 kilometres every day. Sometimes we talked to German soldiers we met and found that their documents were very similar to ours. The rain had stopped, but our shoes were still wet through and our feet were tired and covered in blisters. There were no surviving houses in the village we passed through; the Russians had supposedly destroyed them all deliberately. They had wanted to create two uninhabitable strips of land 50 kilometres wide on both sides of the Oder. We wanted to go around Berlin from the north and walked quickly so as to reach Bernau, 30 kilometres from our destination, by the evening.

We tried to find some accommodation for the night but were met with refusal three times by the local farmers. The last one showed us a pigsty in which it would have been impossible to either stand or lie down. We could not get any jacket potatoes either. Other Germans seemed to live here. Finally, without asking for permission, we found a spot in a local barn before a little boy arrived and led us to a poor farming family, who, without saying anything, offered us food and a sofa to sleep on. When we refused, the woman made it clear that Russian officers had often stayed there and what was good enough for them was even more so for former German soldiers. We left their house the next morning, full of gratitude. Once again, we realized that only those in need will help others who are also in need. We would not ask for help from any rich people again.

The blisters on our feet slowly burst and began to bleed. We often had to stop to sit for a while on a curb. Our next destination for the day was Oranienburg. People's stories about that town were full of horror; there had been a concentration camp there not so long ago and a famine was taking its deadly toll. Due to the horrors committed there, the people of the town were now deprived of any help.

Before we reached the town itself, we were lucky to get a lift on a horse and cart. We were grateful for the ride because we were slowly losing strength. Some Ukrainians joined us on the way. They were exceptionally well dressed and took no notice of us at all. You could see they really liked the country, whose culture they intended to change. We passed by the partially destroyed concentration camp in Oranienburg, but the infamous place was now adorned with the symbols of the liberators who were now in residence. Red banners flew from the buildings, and the main gate was decorated with colourful garlands. Huge propaganda posters hung here and there.

In the middle of a large square was a red victory column with an enormous gold star on the top, visible from afar. However, it was forbidden to enter the camp, and double guards prevented access to anyone who might be curious.

The cart stopped in the city centre and we had to continue on foot. We passed several Russian officers, who paid no attention to the ragged and exhausted figures walking by. From time to time, trucks decorated with red flags full of men and women travelled through, promoting the ideas of the KPD.[71] They sang and yodelled, looking with hatred at those who did not raise their fists in the air with them in salute. We knew their ideas from before 1933, which were particularly popular in the Ruhr area, but now we only looked anxiously at them, and at each other.

We travelled on further, passing around Kremmen from the south to reach Nauen. We went through the western outskirts of Berlin and saw unusual and unforgettable sights. Russians were now living in the wonderfully furnished apartments of the rich villa districts and were doing well. They had put all the heavy, decorative furniture out in the gardens and were sitting on armchairs in their dirty uniforms, as if they had never done anything else. The best dishes and drinks were out on the tables, and they had taken the best clothes from the wardrobes and were parading around in them. We also saw the short, slant-eyed figures that we had met before. In long shirts, which stuck out from under their uniforms, they rode bicycles and motorbikes through the wide streets like crazy. We realized they obviously liked it in Germany very much and probably would not leave anytime soon. Later, we crossed through rural areas again and managed to eat a wonderful potato salad served by a local housewife. She told us that there were almost no men left in the village, and that even the released prisoners of war had been taken by the GPU.[72] The deportation of all the local youths had caused particular indignation.

We reached Nauen in the evening and spent the night in a barn with other refugees, who told us how being exiled from their homes in East Prussia had interrupted their carefree lives. When we set off the next morning, the radio masts near Nauen guided us on our way. We arrived there around noon and saw how the Russians were systematically dismantling them. Cables, copper, and electronic devices lay in a large pile ready for transportation.

We managed to get some bread from a local bakers. Our feet, already very sore, caused us excruciating pain with every step. Limping, we came to a village where we once again spent the night in a barn. The refugees camping there greeted us with compassion and cooked a few potatoes in their pots for us as a gift. Waldemar suggested we join them and earn some food by helping to pull the carts. We set off together the next day, but after a few kilometres were unable to keep up. We turned south and reached the main road again. On the way we met a woman who told us to hide so that we would not get arrested by the GPU. On a country road, about 100 metres ahead, was a truck with a few men in it. The Russians, with bayonets on the barrels of their rifles, were chasing the villagers ahead of them. When the danger had passed, we moved on. A woman directed us to her husband who was working in the field and offered us some soup and bread with lard. During the meal, two girls approached from a nearby house and asked us to stay an hour longer. They told us about their two fiancées, who, just like us, were wandering somewhere alone. They prepared potato pancakes for us and served them with sugar and coffee with milk. We felt like kings. It had been a long time since we had been welcomed and entertained so well. I read this as another sign of Providence, especially since I celebrated my twenty-fifty birthday on that day. My thoughts were with my relatives as I dreamed of one day telling them about the extraordinary hospitality of our compatriots.

We received a warning not to get too close to Braunschweig [Editor's note – not the town in Lower Saxony, but another with the same name].[73] We were advised not to go through it due to the ongoing dismantling of the large Central German steel factories. A huge prisoner of war camp had been built next to it, and 20,000 prisoners had worked there non-stop. Looking at the map, we calculated that walking around the town would mean an additional 15 kilometres, so despite the warnings, we decided to take a chance. We went through the park, which had been completely destroyed by Nebelwerfer rocket launchers.[74] When we asked for water in a nearby villa, we were served with lunch. Then a peasant took us in his horse cart. He was terribly angry with the German soldiers, believing they were to blame for the town's destruction and wanted to flog every last one of them. Waldemar and I secretly thanked God we had not revealed our origins to him. There were huge posters in town showing lists of Kreisleiters and Gauleiters[75] who had been condemned to death by hanging. We also saw huge inscriptions saying, 'People's Tribunal', and the first scaffolds had already been built in the market square.

We walked through a housing estate occupied by people repatriated from Ukraine. Crowds of German-speaking men and women were sitting or lying around.[76] These hitherto unknown martyrs of the past war were now enjoying the fruits of victory. A bit further along, a great prisoner of war camp began and the street we were walking along now ran straight through it. Our comrades were camped in provisional tents and pits; their faces reflecting their sadness and resignation, troubled by the thought that they were now slaves of this great power. In the distance, on the right, were large plants whose machines had already been transported. Now the prisoners were dismantling and separating the steel structures from the factory halls. We did not feel comfortable walking through the camp, and so pulled our hats over our eyes and tried to walk hunched over. From time to time, one of our comrades sitting on the ground would get up and call out something to us from behind the fence. It hit us like a whip's blow. Ignoring these cries, we stubbornly marched silently forward. We had to. We did not want our fate to be decided there behind the barbed wire. The Russian guards positioned every 20 metres or so on both sides did not react but watched us closely. We had been walking for ten minutes and still could not see the end of the camp. We remembered the warnings of the people we had met before. We knew that every Russian guard had the right to capture someone else after a prisoner had escaped, in order to be able to report the full number of prisoners in his 'charge' in the evening.

As we passed one of the last sentries, he reached for his whistle and gave a sharp, prolonged signal with it. In the next moment, a motorcycle zoomed past. Our hearts stopped for a moment as a vision of a prison flashed before our eyes, but the Russians passed by without paying any attention to us. We did not know what had just happened. It was only when we were far away from the camp that we were able to breathe deeply, wipe the sweat from our foreheads and thank the person watching over us. We had once again put all our cards on the table and succeeded.

There was a fishing village called Plaue[77] 5 kilometres ahead and as it was getting dark, we decided to spend the night there. The people were afraid of the Russians, and it took a long time to persuade a woman to give us refuge in her attic just for one night. First, we washed ourselves thoroughly at the pump. Everyone believed that we were all 19 years old and had never been in the army. We looked so much younger after a shave. Next, we bandaged our feet. They looked horrible; puss-filled with raw meat sticking out from our injured, worn-down heels.

We still did not give up. We wanted so much to rest for few days, but the anxiety caused by the presence of the Russians prevented us from stopping. Every day it took us at least a quarter of an hour to put on our shoes on our heavily bandaged feet. We stood on the main road and looked longingly into the distance. Magdeburg lay 80 kilometres ahead of us. Suddenly, an empty truck stopped next us and a Russian lieutenant leaned out of the cab, asking if the road led to Magdeburg. While I tried to explain the way, Waldemar asked him directly if he would like to take us with him. In a moment we were sitting on the back of the truck and speeding quickly along. From time to time,

I pointed the way to the driver, for which he kindly thanked me by nodding his head. Waldemar laughed. He knew I did not know the route at all but was simply reading the yellow signposts in German.

We moved fast. Then the driver braked sharply and it turned out that we were on the outskirts of a town near the former border of the British sector. After the custom officers had checked the driver's documents, the barriers rose and we were approaching Magdeburg. We waited anxiously to cross the Elbe. We had heard that the bridge over the river was closed for civilians and soon saw with our own eyes that it was true. Huge masses of people, mainly refugees with their belongings, were crowded on the riverbanks. The barrier was down and Russian soldiers checked our driver's documents again. One of the guards climbed up and gestured that we should leave the vehicle. However, our driver explained to him that we were his employees and so had to go into town with him. It was close call, and everything nearly ended badly for us. Now, almost screaming with joy, we passed the first and second bridges. Moments later, the car stopped in the town centre. We jumped out, grabbed our hats and extended our hands to the Russian officer in a cordial gesture. He smiled back and drove away.

We were overjoyed. Not only would we have needed at least two days to reach the river, but we would have then had to stand there by the bridge not knowing what to do. We took the tram through Magdeburg to investigate the possibility of crossing the border in the evening. The summer heat had been exhausting, and on that day, 3 August, the sun was shining above us as a symbol of our longed-for freedom.

We stood on the rear platform of the carriage and tilted our hats in a jaunty manner, pulling them down over our ears. We looked like vagabonds in this great city; you would think that just by looking at our clothes. But when we had returned home, we would finally look human again. Those returning from the border brought incredible news. Each had their own way of crossing it, but they also said that everything looked normal in the West. Someone from Cologne said that everyone had enough to eat, that they had a radio, read newspapers every day and went to the cinema. We could not believe it. Yet despite all this we were happy to hear such news and dreamed that it would be just like that for us. We were surprised by the openness and kindness of the people living there, who did everything to help us. In the evening we arrived in Voelpke, where we ate at one of the peasants' homes and took stock of the situation. Apparently, a Frenchman drove across the border every now and then in a truck and took someone with him every time. It seemed unlikely, however, that he would want to take us. We also received a message that the Russians had shot two sailors who were trying to sneak over the border through a cornfield. Such news kept us from moving on that night. We instead spent it in a stable and at dawn on 4 August, we visited a miner who lived in the Soviet occupied zone and worked in a lignite mine in the British zone. I gave him my watch and a ring and asked him to take us with him. He refused to accept the items and, laughing, declared that it was a matter of honour for him, and that he would help us without requiring payment. He thought for a moment and promised that we would cross the border together at 14.00. The guards knew him well and never asked for any documentation. He gave me his English/Russian ID card, while Waldemar received another from the miner's friend who would go with us. We admired their courage and confidence and were touched that they wanted to help us so much.

Our final risky venture thus began. We were fully aware that after overcoming this great obstacle, we would achieve our desired goal and find ourselves in the safe arms of our western homeland. With beating hearts, we rapidly approached the border of both sectors. People stood in line on the right and left, looking at us with amazement and asking if we were soldiers. Without stopping, we pushed through them with determination in our hearts and faith in the success of our bold plan.

THE HUNTED

We were summoned by a guard standing in a booth on the left. We approached and told him we were miners. There was a red barrier in front of us and two more armed Russians next to it, guarding the passage. We freely took off our hats and shook hands in greeting. They responded with a firm hug and then asked for our documents. They did not look at my folded ID card, while Waldemar, in his nervousness, almost forgot to take his out. The asked us why we were not going to work on bicycles, and we replied that they had been stolen by Italian soldiers. The Russians laughed, slapping their hands on their thighs, saying: 'Comme ci, comme ça, they took the machine'. We nodded with a laugh and passed around the barrier. There was another, identical one 50 metres away, but this one was British and was painted with blue, white and red stripes. However, there was no guard this time. We walked on a bit more, then took a deep breath and sat down on the curb for a while. We wiped the sweat from our foreheads and shook hands silently. Our lips quietly uttered the words: 'Thank God'. Our miner friends congratulated us on our success. We gave the ID cards back to them and they show us the way to Helmstedt, from where we could reach Hanover by train.

Back Home

We felt confident on the way to the station in Helmstedt. As always, we looked carefully left and right to see if there were any Russians nearby. From time to time, however, we only met Englishmen in their fast cars. The refugees gathered in large numbers at the station. There was talk here and there about crossing the border. We heard the most unbelievable things. Apparently, the success of the crossing depended on whichever Russian was stood on the border. We also found out that a few days earlier, a few former soldiers had given vodka to the Russians. The custom officers had proceeded to get drunk and then opened the barrier. We felt satisfied with this news. Crowds of people from all sides gathered there for hours. We were angered when we heard a story about a woman who had offered the customs officer 200 cigarettes, but instead of allowing her to pass, he had kicked her.

In the afternoon, we boarded the train heading west. It was supposed to take us to Braunschweig first. We saw our first Americans and even Negroes. How great was our surprise at the sight of German women walking arm in arm with them. In the train compartment, a smartly dressed man gave us a slice of bread and butter. We felt enormous gratitude and were filled with joy to be returning to our homeland. In Braunschweig, we were directed to a bunker for the night, where, after soup and coffee served by the sisters from the German Red Cross, we entered a room with two bunks. While I laid down and dreamed about meeting my loved ones, Waldemar constantly circled the room. After a while, he came up to me holding two pieces of paper in his raised hand. It turned out that he had received two tickets from his sister to travel to West Germany. I could not believe it.

Only when I held the tickets in my hands and looked at Waldemar's beaming face, bursting with laughter at my amazement, did I come to my senses. He had had another wonderful idea.

The truck was to leave from the agreed location at 07.00 on 6 August 1945. We could not sleep a wink that night, as we dreamed about the future in joyful excitement. We wondered what it would be like when we reached home. Waldemar said that if our families knew we were so close by, they would not be able to sleep either. Long ahead of the required time, we were already stood at the meeting point, waiting for the truck to come. The time dragged on mercilessly. We learned from the other refugees that our transport was going all the way to Aachen. I wondered if the truck would pass through my hometown of Bochum. It was 08.00, then 09.00. Just as some of us were losing hope, a truck with a trailer pulled up at the corner of the street. We got in immediately. There were about 100 of us and we would all have to stand up, but what did that matter? We approached Hannover. At 12.00, we stopped to refuel at a large petrol station on the edge of town. The sun broke through the clouds and enveloped us in its warmth as we drove fast along a motorway.

How differently we had imagined the way west. Two days before we had debated walking north or south from the motorway, but now we were riding on it. Everyone's faces were happy to be going home. What would the reunion with our loved ones look like? We all asked ourselves this question. We were fast approaching the industrial areas. Our documents were checked in Herford and Bielefeld, and together with Waldemar, we passed these checks successfully. Now we could see the smoking chimneys from the factories in Hamm.

We passed the town from the south and continued along the motorway towards the Ruhr. We were going so fast we reached the outskirts of Dortmund in the late afternoon. On the left and right we saw rubble that we remembered well from other towns. We saw people dressed in their best clothes walking down the streets. It was a Sunday, but we had already forgotten about this mood because no one celebrated Sundays in the Soviet zone. People had to work in the fields regardless of the day of the week. We were even surprised to see dancing couples in a beer garden. Travellers who had already reached their destination gradually left the truck, and I asked the driver if he would be going through Bochum. He replied that he would not be going to the centre, but would cross the Bochum-Riemke district. I was so excited that I could not remember which side these districts were on.

The truck stopped at the intersection. After such a long drive, we could not find our balance on the solid ground. Waldemar had already decided that he would go with me to my parent's house first. As I wondered what to do next, he stopped a passing car, so we got in and after a while were in the town centre. We felt very uncomfortable sitting on the car seats in our torn clothes. There were a lot of people at the tram stop, all smartly dressed. We felt ashamed when they looked at us, and they even moved away from us on the tram. We must have looked like Poles for them to react to us in that way.[78] Half an hour later we reached my home district.

We had to walk for half an hour to reach my parents' house. How often had I walked along that road, but the situation that day was special. As we got closer to our destination, we quickened our pace despite our injured feet. I was constantly telling Waldemar about all the familiar places, showing him the Ruhr Valley and the small town of Blankenstein in the distance. Every element of the landscape, every surviving house was a ray of joy for my longing soul. How often had I passed that way, but never before had that road been so beautiful and joyous as it was on that Sunday evening.

It was after 20.00 and the sun was sinking below the horizon. We were only a few hundred metres from my house, but I could not see it yet. We fell silent and walked even faster. The bridge over the Ruhr had been destroyed, but the house itself, thank God, was still standing. I breathed a sigh of relief. A few more steps. 'My God, please let my parents be safe and sound,' I prayed. The neighbours downstairs had locked the door for fear of Poles plundering the area. They opened it to us in amazement, and, accompanied by Waldemar, I went up the stairs to my parents' apartment.

This was the moment I had been waiting for for so long. I felt dizzy. I instinctively knocked on the door and entered the room. My father was sitting at the table and my mother looked at me inquiringly. 'Good evening, mother,' I said and then she recognized me. What happened next was unimaginable. We were overcome by a wave of deep emotion. What Waldemar witnessed was not just a homecoming, it was a resurrection. The reaching of the goal for which we had fought like lions. My God, we had done it. Everything around us was so beautiful. So beautiful. My mother continued to hug me to her heart. When they had heard the last report from Poznań on the radio, they thought I had died. Yet here I was with them. It took a long time before my ailing father could understand that I was back with him again. His health had deteriorated significantly. I remembered their pain when they had bid me farewell as I left for military school, and I remembered my father crying with despair as I shook his hand for the last time.

As my mother lay the table with all the finest specialties hidden in the cupboards and cellar, the neighbours notified my fiancée that I had returned. If we had arrived half an hour earlier, we would have met her there as she had come to visit my parents. After a while, her brother entered the room to see for himself that I had survived. We never wanted to return to Poznań again. We were happy to be alive together. The heavens opened for me and my fiancée, as I greeted the person who had always believed in me and had not lost hope that I had survived. My God, life should only consist of moments like that. Later on, Waldemar and I told them everything we had experienced, as we recreated our journey back to our homeland.

With my mind's eye I saw Poznań again, for which we had fought such fierce battles. We remembered the moment we had broken out of it, our march west and all the hours of heroism that until then no one had known about. Full of pride, we told them about our last days in the forest in Rohrfort and talked about our 'last battalion' with a smile. Then, in all its glory, was the moment when we took off our grey uniforms, laid down our weapons and surrendered to Providence. I had not lost my faith and had fulfilled my duty!

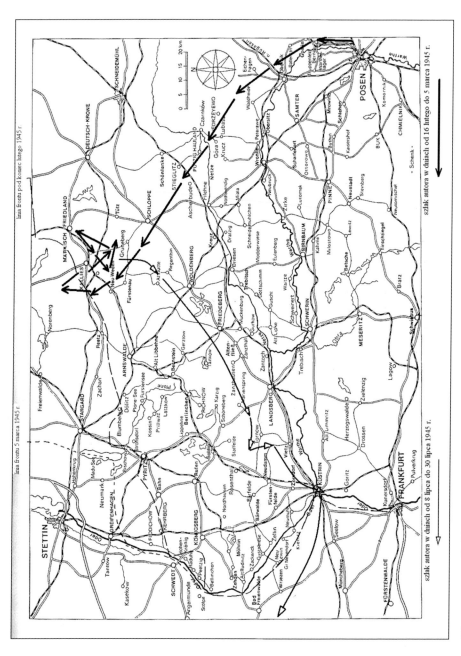

The route travelled by Hans Klapa and his companions from 16 February to 30 July 1945.

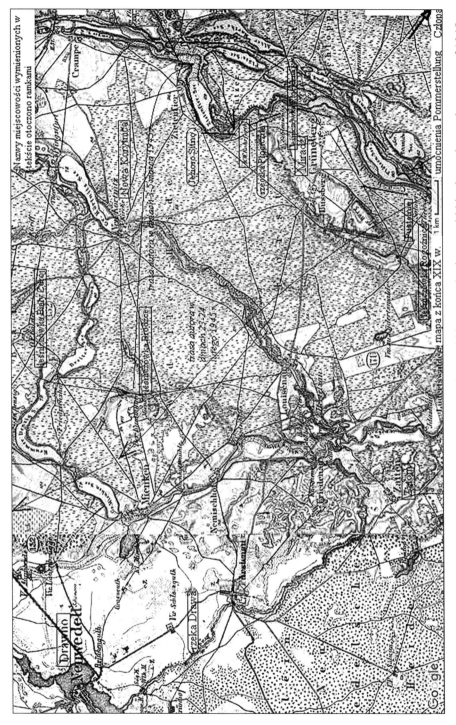

The area covered by the Drawski National Park, where the author and his comrades in arms hid in the spring and summer of 1945.

Notes

1. Such statements may arouse justified indignation in Polish (and other European) readers, who are aware not only of Soviet but also numerous German crimes committed during the Second World War. We do not know how aware the author was of such things, since he could not possibly have known of all the atrocities committed by the German Army during the war. Hans Klappa was 25 years old in 1945. He read *Mein Kampf* every day and was most probably unaware of the numerous German crimes previously committed in the conquered and occupied territories. The Nuremberg Trials did not take place until after the war, and even then, the German people still did not believe everything the witnesses described.

2. This conviction was common among German soldiers fighting on the Eastern Front in the last months of the Second World War (including the German editor). However, he either forgets or does not want to remember that the war began six years earlier, with Germany's aggression against Poland, and the events of 1944-45 were, in a way, the aftermath of the conquest, terror and occupation of the countries invaded by the Third Reich.

3. It is hard to say what the author had in mind when writing about a 'successful' fight. Did he mean the German Army's almost month-long resistance against the Red Army, the result of which meant that several Soviet divisions heading towards the River Oder were held up, even if this was at the cost of several thousand dead and wounded and would lead to eventual defeat? Or was

he referring to his own actions, which, thanks to his personal courage, luck and a strong will to survive, led him to the ultimate success: his own survival?

4. Baroness Marie von Ebner-Eschenbach (née Dubsky) (1830-1916) was born in the Czech Republic to a mixed Czech-Saxon family. An Austrian author, she is counted among the great German-language writers of the late nineteenth century. Known for her deep psychological novels and beautiful style, her works address the contemporary problems of her time, particularly social issues. She preached the ideas of human love, regardless of nationality and religion. The quote probably comes from a very popular work *Aphorismen* (Aphorisms), published in German in 1880, 1884, 1890, 1893, 1921 and 1971. German editions were added to over time and the 1974 edition contained 675 aphorisms. The Polish edition of 1974 included only 378, some of which were never published in the German originals, and were probably taken from her previous works. The 'missing' 329 can be found in the *Fronda* magazine (No.36, 2005), translated by Michał Wojciechowski.

   It is not known what Hans Klapa meant when he said that these words by Ebner-Eschenbach gave the men the 'courage and enthusiasm to fight'. Perhaps her sayings were used in publications read at German cadet schools or in other propaganda. This was all the more likely as Ebner-Eschenbach's husband, Feldmarschallleuntant Moritz von Ebner-Eschenbach (1815-1898) was an Austrian military engineer who was an outstanding inventor and a long-time professor and vice-chancellor at a Viennese engineering academy. The military education of a Third Reich soldier often referred to the traditions of an Austrian education.

5. The Wehrmacht's 5th Infantry Cadet School in Poznań (Schule V für Fahnenjunker der Infanterie Posen), whose commander at the time was Oberst Ernst Gonell.

6. The author, perhaps influenced by propaganda, uses the expression 'great German city' several times when referring to Poznań, which, for obvious reasons, may arouse justified objections from the Polish reader.
7. The training ground and military camp at Biedrusko (Truppenubungplatz 'Warthelager') was where part of the 5th Wehrmacht Infantry Cadet School was located.
8. The station was in nearby Bolechowo, about 2 km from the training camp, on the east bank of the River Warta, which had to be crossed on the way to the camp.
9. The cadet school was divided into inspections corresponding to the size of a company, and these in turn were divided into units the size of a platoon. There were nine inspections in Biedrusko, with another four at the Golęcin barracks in Poznań.
10. During the later battles for Poznań, Major Eberhard Hahn would command the 'Warta' Sector (Abschnitt 'Warthe'), one of the three main sectors (in addition to the 'East' (Abschnitt 'Ost') and 'West' (Abschnitt 'West') in the German defence system of Fortress Poznań (Festung Posen).
11. During the later battles for Poznań, Fritz Heinemann, already a Hauptmann [captain], commanded a company of heavy weapons in the northeast of the city, as part of Subsection III.
12. A student at German military schools.
13. In the areas incorporated into the Third Reich, ie the so-called 'Warta Country', with its capital in Poznań, the Polish police (known as the 'navy-blue') were not retained in the way the occupier did in the General Government. It is difficult to determine what armed officer the author is referring to here. Perhaps he meant a German policeman or factory worker, who, being a Volksdeutsche or Baltic German, spoke little German. Perhaps he was a member of the Forstschutzkommando (Forestry Protection Commando), which was subordinate to Göring, and consisted of uniformed and armed forestry workers, 2,000 of whom were sent

to the territories in occupied Poland in 1939. It is most likely, however, that the forests around Biedrusko were protected by the Wehrmacht's forestry service.

14. The size of the German garrison stationed in Poznań during the occupation was overestimated by the author.

15. The original *Der Mythus des 20. Jahrhunderts* (Myth of the Twentieth Century), published in 1930, was written by one of the best-known works of the main Nazi ideologists Alfred Rosenberg (1893-1946). It contained, among other racist theories, the idea that National Socialism was the goal of humanity and would bring victory in the eternal struggle to the Aryan people (the only ones able to create culture) over the Jews, who the author placed lower on the cultural ladder. Beginning in the nineteenth century with the anti-Catholic Kulturkampf offensive of Reich Chancellor Bismarck, 'political Catholicism' was used in Germany to the activity and independent attitude of the Roman Catholic Church, which was treated as a German institution, but subordinated to foreign management in Rome/the Vatican and therefore not subject to the control of the German state.

16. Treskau is the German name of the village of Owińska, near Poznań, where there was a Cistercian nunnery with a huge estate. After the Second Partition of Prussia and the dissolution of the Order, the Prussian authorities sold the property to a Berlin banker and supplier of the manor, Zygmunt Otton von Treskow, whose numerous descendants divided the land among themselves. In 1904, the two von Treskow brothers sold the area of Biedrusko to the Prussian Army for a training ground and training camp called Warthelager, but until 1945 the family owned the neighbouring estates in Radojewo and Owińska.

    The author probably means Jona von Treskow (1892-1975), the widow of the owner, or Hellen Margarethe Hedwig von Treskow (1882-1952), the wife of the last owner of the estate in Radojewo, Hermann Otto Hugo von Treskow (1872 -1939), who was interned by Poles as an ethnic German and shot dead during transportation in Koło on 11 September 1939.

17. Festung Saint Nazaire, part of so-called Atlantic Wall, intended to defend the French coast against an Allied invasion. It was organized around the port city in southern Brittany and over vast areas to the north of the Loire estuary, beginning from February 1944. Fortress St. Nazaire, however, was not stormed and the Allies were instead content to blockade it, unlike Brest and Cherbourg. Thirty thousand German soldiers held out in St. Nazaire from 5 August 1944 until its surrender on 11 May 1945.

18. This included the 500th Assault Gun Training and Reserve Battalion (Sturmgeschütz-Ersatz und Ausbildungs-Abteilung 500) stationed in Poznań, in the vicinity of the 5th Infantry Cadet School.

19. Four inspections belonging to the 2nd Training Group (Lehrgruppe), stationed in the barracks at Poznań Golęcin (Kuhndorf barracks). The remaining 1st and 3rd Training Groups consisted of eight inspections (1st-4th and 9th-12th) and an additional 13th Inspection, and were stationed in Biedrusko.

20. This name was taken from the military unit of Tsarist Russia. A corps with this name fought during the Russo-Japanese War (1904-1905), and then from 1914-1917 on the Narew and in Lithuania during the First World War.

21. Most likely at the airport in Kobylnica.

22. The construction of eighteen forts (nine main ones and nine smaller ones) around Poznań took place in two stages and lasted from 1876 to 1896.

23. The citadel in Poznań, which before (and for part of) the Second World War was known as Fort Winiary but was renamed Kernwerk in 1943 or 1944.

24. Unfortunately, as far as we know, no film or photographic materials from these manoeuvres exists. Perhaps they were never actually published or were lost during the war.

25. No sources confirm that Reichsführer SS Heinrich Himmler (then the formal commander of the so-called Wehrmacht Reserve Army) and General Heinz Guderian (Chief of Staff of the German High Command) took part in these manoeuvres. Himmler was also formally commander of Army Group 'Upper Rhine' on the Western Front until 22 January 1945 and was most likely at its command post. However, in the second half of January 1945, he received an order to form Army Group 'Wisł' in Pomerania, and travelled there in the fourth week of January.

    When writing his memoires, the author probably remembered being told about Himmler and Guderian's presence at the Volksturm parade in Poznań on 6 November 1944, therefore mixing up both these events.

26. The author is referring to the 4th Infantry Cadet School at Toruń, the sister school of the 5th Infantry Cadet School. However, the siege of the German fortress at Toruń by the Red Army took place on 26 January 1945 and finished during the night of 30/31 January after the withdrawal of the German garrison to the west, beyond the Vistula.

27. Dating back to the time of the partitions, the barracks of the Prussian 6th Regiment of Grenadiers, named after Graf Kleist von Nollendorf (1. West Prussian), was at Szylinga Street. After the Greater Poland Uprising (1918-1919), they were transferred to the 57th Greater Poland Infantry Regiment. The City Police Headquarters are currently located there.

28. The author was in the 'Hamel' Battalion, under Major Franz Hamel, in the third sub-section of Poznań Fortress.

29. This number was greatly exaggerated or is a mistake in the text. In reality there were eight German anti-aircraft batteries with 88-mm guns in the battle for Poznań, including three double batteries, so in all about forty guns and a number of smaller calibre artillery.

30. The author rightly stipulates that the date in his calendar may be inaccurate. In fact, the 'Hamel' Battalion (according to its

records) occupied a position on the right bank in Poznań, and the assault of the Soviet armoured forces on Swarzędz took place on 22 January 1945.

31. The so-called Subsection III of the Poznań Fortress. It is otherwise difficult to understand the use of the term 'regiment' here. Its equivalents in the fortress's structures were subsections consisting of two battalions and other smaller units, just like a regiment.

32. The landing strip at the Zeppelin hall at Winiary, Poznań, which was under fire but did not prevent German planes from landing there until 5 February 1945.

33. The author is referring to the Soviet IS-2 heavy tank (Josef Stalin 2), which was armed with a long-barrelled 122-mm gun.

34. The neighbouring (right-wing) battalion within Subsection III was the 'Styx' Battalion, commanded by Hauptmann Hans Styx, who were manning Fort IIIa. This fort, or part of it, had been stormed by Red Army soldiers on 29 January 1945, which resulted in the need to strengthen the battalion.

35. The correct name of the mill in the Nadolnik district, on the River Główna.

36. The term 'regiment's headquarters' actually means the headquarters of Subsection III of the fortress, located in the 'Nivea' factory. However, this was the same subsection to which the 'Hamel' Battalion, in which the author served, was stationed.

37. The author is referring to the defence of the Metz Fortress on the Western Front in September and October 1944 by alarm units formed by the Junkers of the VI Infantry Cadet School in Metz. Their participation in the fighting and their commendation of a special armband (Metz 1944) was publicised by the German propaganda machine. After the evacuation of the Western Front in January 1945, the school was stationed in Międzyrzecz, in today's Lubuska region.

38. Major Rudolf Michel was the commander of Subsection III.

39. Werner Spille was a company commander in the right-wing 'Styx' Battalion of Subsection III.

40. During the siege of Poznań, Koppert was the commander of a platoon of heavy infantry guns in the 'Hamel' Battalion.

41. The place where they crossed the River Noteć was probably lock No. 16 in Pianówka, near Czarnków, or lock No. 17, located 5 km further west, in Mikołajów.

42. The author was probably aware that part of the population of northern Greater Poland was created following the wartime immigration of German settlers brought from the Black Sea (Bessarabia) in 1940, and that a large part of the natives were Poles. However, he only states very cautiously that Black Sea Germans live there and a moment later calls them 'natives'.

43. A village on the southern section of the fortification line, the so-called 'Pomeranian Wall', about 30 kilometres to the west. However, the information obtained by the author was incorrect as the position near Stare Osieczno was stormed by Soviet armoured units as early as 28 January 1945. On 20 February, the Germans attempted an unsuccessful counter-offensive from Pomerania to the south on the section from Kalisz Pomorski to the Oder. The front in those days – around 21 February – was already based on the Oder in the west, and in the north ran approximately along the line Kalisz Pomorski - Choszczno – Pyrzyce. The nearest German positions were therefore about 50 kilometres to the northwest, just near Kalisz Pomorski, which was captured by the Red Army on 12 February.

44. Górnica is situated about 10 kilometres southwest from Trzcianka. In the original manuscript, the author misspelled the name of the village as Gornitz.

45. Drawno had been in Soviet hands for at least ten days, and the German troops counter-attacking from the north (Operation 'Sonnenwende') on 15-20 February failed to reach Drawno from the northwest. However, it cannot be ruled out that the

rear Soviet defensive line was located on the line of the River Drawa, hence the particular saturation of the described area with Red Army troops. If the author had managed to cross the Drawa, the German positions would have been about 10 kilometres northwest of Drawno.

46. Most likely the double bridge crossing the Drawa, on the Wałcz-Szczecin road, near Prostynia (Wildforth). Until 1945 it was known as the Laatziger Brucke and was captured by the Red Army on 12 February, or a few days later.

47. In those days, there was indeed a frontline in the northern outskirts of the town of Prostynia, about 1 km from the Laatziger Brücke. On 1 March 1945, a great Soviet offensive of the 1st Belorussian Front started north from this border, which was to lead to the capture of the entire Pomeranian region. The composition of the striking troops included the 1st Guards Tank Army of General Katukov, which attacked and bypassed Poznań in the last week of January.

48. In this area, the Drawa flows from north to south. The author was moving north, following the Soviet attack that began on 1 March 1945.

49. German volunteer units of a reactionary and counter-revolutionary character, formed after the defeat of Germany in the First World War due to the disintegration of the former Imperial Army. In 1919, these units fought against the revolution in Germany and fought on the eastern border of Germany with Polish pro-independence fighters.

50. The author is probably trying to refer to Soviet propaganda messages, which he had come across at the end, or rather after the end of the war. Meanwhile, it was the Germans who had started and waged the war in the name of their alleged cultural superiority. It is therefore surprising that years later, such sentiment should be attributed to the Soviet side, and the author's indignation seems rather theatrical.

51. The partly autobiographical book *Menschen, die gejagt warden: Aus meinem Leiben* was published in Berlin in 1938 under the penname of Tex Harding. In a book combining memories and reportage, the author describes the adventures of a young gunslinger from the underworld of Bogota, who in recognition of his shooting skills, was engaged by Colombian police to a special search and investigation group to prosecute extremely dangerous criminals. The Austrian author's real name was Heinrich Peskoller (1898 or 1902-1940?) As a teenager, Peskoller escaped to Brazil before the First World War, where he became an adventurer, cowboy and traveller across the Americas. After returning to Austria in 1931, he started his writing career and published several crime and adventure novels under pseudonyms. Following the defeat of France in 1940, he tried to interest the Reich Main Security Office in the conquest of French Guyana.

52. In the areas described on the approach to Mirosławiec, there were no fortifications belonging to the Pomeranian Wall, whose main position was located about 15 km south. However, these were probably field fortifications, road barriers and trenches made during fighting of winter 1945. Mirosławiec was captured on 10 February by Polish units of the 1st Polish Army, which from 1 March also participated in the offensive towards the north.

53. Probably the now non-existent Rohrbuch forester's lodge, located about 2 km northeast of Biały Zdrój.

54. The River Stawica (Teich Fliess), which flows into Lake Wieliż (Grosser See).

55. Probably one of the now non-existent Balster or Griff forester's lodges, south of Lake Wieliż.

56. The now non-existent bridges over the branches of the River Płociczna (Plotzenfliess), about 1 km east of the former village of Zietenfier, north of Lake Sitno (Zientefier-See).

57. The described buildings are the former Heidchen forester's lodge and the nearby Rohrforth gamekeeper's cottage on the River

Płociczna, which flows from Lake Sitno (from its southwestern edge). The buildings were located in the northern part of the current Drawa National Park.

58. Probably a former forester's lodge located 1 km northeast of Miradz (Grüneberg) in the Płociczna Valley.

59. The battle for Kassel in central Germany took place from 1-4 April 1945. The German garrison, mobilized in emergency mode, had unexpectedly put up a strong resistance in the ruins of the repeatedly bombarded town against the 80th US Infantry Division of the XX Corps of General Patton's 3rd Army. The fierce resistance of the Germans, reinforced with tanks and anti-aircraft artillery, failed to minimize the numerical and material superiority of the Americans and to save Kassel from capitulation. The Battle of the Ruhr began on 22 March with the Americans crossing the Rhine north of Düsseldorf and south of Cologne, which led to the complete encirclement of German Army Group B in the Ruhr on 1 April. The liquidation of the encircled German forces continued until 18 April, ending with the capture of 325,000 prisoners of war.

60. Reitzenstein was likely the family name of the rich German landowners to whom the surrounding estate belonged.

61. The described event took place after the German surrender, which the members of the group knew about, meaning that this is a description of a war crime, completely unjustified by the rules of warfare. According to the terms of Germany's unconditional surrender of 8 May 1945, every German soldier or officer caught with a weapon after this date was treated as a bandit. Due to the awareness of the end of the war, such incidents cannot be classified and treated differently – the described group of German marauders also committed other attacks, murders and common crimes that cannot be classified as military (soldierly) activity.

62. The described incident should be classified as a criminal lynching of German marauders on an alleged Russian deserter.

63. Probably Markisch-Friedland (Mirosławiec).

64. Probably the former Schwanenfeld forester's lodge, 350 metres east of the Jeziorki Wałeckie train station on the Wałcz – Szczecin line.

65. A now non-existent mill on the River Runica (Kuhnowfliess), about 2.5 km northeast of Lake Sitno and about 4 km west of Tuczno.

66. Author error. Taking into account the route described, it was the road from Gorzów Wielkopolski to Szczecin.

67. Author error. Taking into account the route described, it was a forest complex north of Gorzów Wielkopolski, 50 km from the Oder.

68. The only lake in this area is Lake Marwicko (Steg-See), 12 km northwest of Gorzów Wielkopolski. The aforementioned 'forester's lodge' was the now non-existent fishing settlement of Marwitzer Fischers.

69. A village in the Lubiszyn commune, about 20 km northwest of Gorzów Wielkopolski and 30 km from the Oder, near Kostrzyn.

70. In Mosina (Messin) and the nearby village of Tarnówek (Splinterfelde) were working subcamps for French and Soviet prisoners of war from Stalag IIIC – Alt Drewitz (now Kostrzyn-Drzewice).

71. Kommunistische Partei Deutschlands [German Communist Party].

72. The author uses an anachronistic name for the Soviet security authorities. The GPU [Gosudarstwiennoje Politiczeskoje Uprawlenije] were the political police who dealt with intelligence, counterintelligence, public security, and border control in Soviet Russia from 1921-22. From 1923-34 it functioned under the name of the OGPU [Objedinionnoje Gosudarstwiennoje Politiczeskoje Uprawlenije], and in 1934 was transformed and incorporated into the NKVD- People's Commissariat of Internal Affairs. It is not clear from the context if the author is referring to the Soviet military counter-intelligence or the NKVD.

73. The author means Brandenburg.

74. It is not known on what basis the author determined the reasons for the park's destruction. Perhaps he had noticed tracks characteristic of the German Nebelwerfer, which meant there would have been a firing position in the park. If he was only judging it on the number of craters caused by explosions, then several other types of artillery could have been responsible.

75. Terms for German NSDAP party officers who managed a county (Kreis) or district (Gau).

76. Most likely ethnic Germans repatriated from Ukraine.

77. Near Brandenburg an der Harvel.

78. The author is referring to the forced labourers from Poland who were badly treated in Germany and therefore were much more poorly dressed than the Germans.

How I Became a Fighter for Poznań

Memoires of an Assault Gun Crew Member

Alfred Kriehn

My field brigade was stationed in Rössel [Reszel] in East Prussia during Christmas and New Year of 1944. If someone had told me then about Poznań, I would have just shaken my head. At that time Poznań was for the front units, which were still in the area around Warsaw, on the Vistula River, out of reach. The brigade had only three guns left, which were used to capture territory in Latvia and had since become unusable again. The rest, which were stuck in Memel [Kłajpeda, Lithuania], were handed over to relieve another brigade that had been transferred from Courland. Our brigade was transferred by sea, without guns, to Pilau and Königsberg [Królewiec].

During the stormy sea crossing to Pilau, I spent half a night sitting in the forecastle of our 5,000-ton ship at the anchor capstan. The air in the hold was terrible. Half the crew below decks were seasick and vomited whenever and whatever they could. At least the weather was unfavourable to hostile submarines, although we did not realize this at the time.

From what I remember, the alarm was sounded early in the morning of 16 January 1945. The battery stood ready to fight in front of our office headquarters, near the railway station. The duty officer was a senior, highly decorated Wachtmeister of our battery, with whom I, a young Gefreiter, had had a terrible run in with a few days earlier, which did not bode well at all. Our battery had reported to the Wachtmeister, and with his thick notebook in hand, he had walked along the line, stopping in front of me to say: 'Gefreiter Kriehn will report immediately to Unteroffizier O. He needs a loader!'

'Yes, Herr Wachtmeister!'

I slung my rifle, picked up the packages, took two steps forward, stood to attention and reported: 'Gefreiter Kriehn checking out!'

'Come on, come on, hurry up, they're already at the loading dock!'

I want to add that after I had turned around and made a hasty retreat, I never saw any of my colleagues from the 1st Battery again, especially two of my comrades-in-arms, whom I had been with since our initial recruitment in September 1943 until that moment. My later attempts to obtain information about them from the Red Cross have, so far, been unsuccessful.

Earlier, however, after all vacationers had left, part of the unit was dispatched to Burg, near Magdeburg, to pick up new guns. These forty-three new guns – each with a two-man crew – were on their way to East Prussia, but never reached the brigade. Eight of these guns were later used in Poznań, but I will return to this later. My gun was on the wagon, so I managed to find an axe and fastened the gun to the tracks with a rope and then nailed it to the floor of the cart.

Shortly afterwards, the transport moved towards Allenstein [Olsztyn] and then further south along the curve of the River Vistula. The next night, after reaching Kutno between 22.00 and 24.00, we received the order to unload. The time passed quickly. In less than an hour, the whole battery was stood on the loading ramp or in the grounds of the railway station and the gun commanders were called to receive their orders. The engines fired up and everyone set off. When leaving the station, the vehicles turned left. Just like before, I never saw any of these machines or the men inside them again. They went west.

The three guns that turned right were led by Oberleutnant Hallmann. Together with his Kübelwagen driver, he knew that the most difficult task during the retreat would be refuelling the vehicles. It was not his fault that he would be unsuccessful, but no one knew this at the time. Later, in Poznań, it was my unit's task to bury him in the Citadel. Hallmann had a truck with fuel and ammunition. The platoon commander of these three guns was an Oberwachtmeister with many years of experience. A few kilometres east of Kutno, we took up lodgings on the outskirts of some estate, relatively far away in a park. We received orders to prepare to march to the German headquarters stationed in this property and to cover the columns during the march. To this day, I still wonder what they were doing that required all night to pack up. When we received orders, it took us 1-2 hours at most, but hardly ever that long. Meanwhile, we simply waited there and had a peaceful and memorable night.

We took up our position near a hill that sloped gently eastward. The bottom of the valley at the foot of the hill was invisible in the darkness. It was probably a little swampy; there was definitely a stream down there. The opposite slope rose just as gently before us, showing ploughed farmland gently dusted with snow. On the hill ahead of us – about 2 kilometres away – we could see in the darkness a road emerging from another valley on the right. It continued over the hill before disappearing behind another hill to the left of us. It was some time before we noticed this, and for a very simple reason: part of the Red Army's offensive unfolded before our very eyes that night.

Fully illuminated, it moved forward: trucks, then a short break, and then more vehicles, artillery, and infantry, all with the crunch of caterpillar tracks in between. The wind was really bad, and we only heard scraps of noise from time to time, sometimes just single, indistinct noises, but we could always see the lights of the motorized column. They were not afraid of an air attack – much less one at night. Who among us could do them any harm? All this took place in a very spooky setting, but we watched on regardless…

At dawn, the road was suddenly deserted. One column had disappeared to the left, and no one was coming towards us from the right. However, those on the other side could see us. They looked at us carefully. After a while, three Russian armoured guns appeared. They turned off the road into the fields and crossed the opposite slope. They must have seen the swampy ground as we watched them travel along its banks in our direction.

They showed us half of the front and half the right flank of their column. We stretched our position a little and grouped two 7.5-cm guns on the left and right, with our 10.5-cm howitzer in between. At the time, this was a very popular addition to assault gun brigades.

I cannot remember the names of our gun commanders. They worked by calling out their first names, having known each other for so long.

'Karl!' A voice from the left would shout. 'You take the first one, I'll take the second. My first shot means "open fire", is that clear?'

'Sure, Gustav!'

'The howitzer should wait. I'll fire to 800 metres, but the howitzer should only fire, if necessary, at 600 metres!'

'Got it!'

And that's how it happened. The three guns crept up in a straight line. 'Boom!' went the first shot, with its neighbour firing almost simultaneously. It did not take long; I think it was the second shot that hit the target. The second enemy gun was hit by the third shot, and each time there was an additional shot to the now-motionless enemy gun, which was slowly burning. The smoke rolled to the side and after a while began to turn red. When a blast of wind blew the dark smoke off to the side, we noticed the third gun, which, following its own tracks, was now retreating. As it reversed, the rear of the vehicle was slightly raised, and its front pointed slightly downwards. A typical example of how armoured vehicles behave when going backwards. 'Butt up, mouth down', as we used to say.

'Gustav', I heard from the right, 'what are we going to do about the third one?' Silence. Then an intriguing answer that I still remember to this day:

'Let him come and report back…!'

And that was that. Believe it or not, the tension among the four of us observers in our howitzer was broken with crazy laughter ('Let him come and report back…!') Perhaps our commander had simply been ordered to save ammunition.

Everything went quiet on the other side. A little later, a liaison officer on a motorbike broke through the field to tell us that his staff was about to leave and that we should cover them for another hour. After less than half an hour, our commander ordered us to march. That should have been enough time for them, and we were slower anyway. For the reminder of the day we headed towards Poznań, but I had no idea which way or how we were going to get there.

After dark, squeezed in various columns, we lost two of our companions. They must have gone left or straight on at some point, while our column went right. We had not slept at all for almost forty hours, and the crews of the armoured vehicles were also exhausted. In one town we passed through, our driver tried to turn left too late and hooked the protruding gun barrel on a telegraph pole. I remember screaming out to warn him, but the sturdy mast had already lifted the barrel slightly off the bearing. The driver turned back so that the zippers retracted, but unfortunately the gun was no longer aligned properly.

Later, we passed an anti-tank ditch made by hard-working engineers in the autumn of 1944.[1] Alongside the road, the ditch was filled in enough for us to cross. Our gun commander probed the left side of the gap, and I probed the right. The caterpillar tracks protruded a few centimetres above the edge of the slope. We took a deep breath as we reached the other side. Luckily, everything was alright, but shortly after this something happened. After passing through a town there was a long bend and the road at this time of night (midnight) was icy. You may not believe it, but armoured vehicles can also slide on ice. We took the turn a little too fast and started to drift until the right track hovered over the sharply sloping escarpment, while the main body of the vehicle sat right on the edge. Initially, the tracks were not stuck out too far, so our driver tried to get back on the road. He almost succeeded. Almost. Decades ago, right in that spot, a conscientious road builder, whatever nationality he was, had placed a solid stone as a mile post. And it was exactly this stone that our right-side gear, i.e. the drive wheel of the right caterpillar track, hit. The driver tried again, but with the same result. Then I heard the driver's voice:

'Herr Unteroffizier, something is wrong with the front crosshead brake on the right and I can't move the right track!'

I was sent to check what was wrong but was unable to see anything in the darkness. Running my hand over the drive wheel all the way to the shaft, I had the impression that the gear was moving forward. If only I could be sure.

We had to stop. If our colleagues had been there, they could have helped us out of such a critical position. But where were they? The driver of our gun finally told me to be on the lookout as he made his way back to the village we had just passed through to reconnoitre our position. After a while, he returned.

'God damn, there's another Leutnant with an infantry company on the radio. He wants us to wait half an hour until the column has passed through. After that, he and his men will get out of here.'

The column went by. I looked down at the tired horses and thickly wrapped figures. Suddenly, I jumped up: 'Herr Unteroffizier, that cart over there disappearing into the darkness, there's a motorbike with a sidecar on it…!'

'Bring the driver here, boy!'

The man with the cart welcomed the opportunity to rest his old horse and walked over to our gun. 'What's up with your machine? Is it broken?'

'No, we've just run out of fuel, sir.' (Winter uniforms come in handy sometimes as they don't reveal any insignia).

'No gas? Well, I'll give you a 20-litre canister, but you'll have to take our loader to Warthbrücken [Koło].'

This was the next town. 'Yes, sir!'

He would get his 20 litres and thus be able to relieve his tired horse. I slung the submachine gun over my shoulder, sat in the passenger's seat and away we went. Only after a while did I discover that the fat bundle in the sidecar, which I had originally mistaken for a sack of potatoes, was in fact the driver's wife, and that he himself was an Hilfspolizei [auxiliary police] officer. My driver dropped me off in the town and, without wasting time waiting for my thanks, headed west.

I stood there with my order: 'Bring me a tractor, boy!' There was a park surrounding me, a church behind me, a faint glow coming through the branches, with mansions on the other side of town, or at least there used to be. There were military signs here and there showing me the way, but the front door of the villa was closed. So, I followed the footprints in the snow that led to the right, to the garden entrance and a double flight of stairs with an unglazed, covered door that stood open. Inside, downstairs, it was pretty quiet. I heard a commotion upstairs, so I followed the sounds upwards. When I opened the door, I was hit by a stench that could be cut with a knife as I entered the former study, which was now the command post of the 2nd "Brandenburg" Regiment.

The liaison officers sat exhausted in their armchairs. You could hear the clatter of typewriters, the voices in the background, and the jingling of telegraphs. An officer was pacing up and down. There was total confusion, and no one seemed to be bothered about my presence at all. It should be noted that in my camouflage uniform, I was no different from the other tired liaison officers. After all, I had not slept for forty-eight hours. Without thinking, I sat down in one of the armchairs, half asleep on the outside, half awake on the inside.

'Tractor! Here? Where? How?'

I lay there with the cigarette smoke, the heat, the stuffiness, the stink of sweat and background voices all around me…The telephone rang: 'Yes, understood, the road to Poznań is blocked, the intersection is under fire, T-34…'

Well, I thought, there are three possibilities: either that Hilfspolizei officer had just arrived, or he was the first to come under fire, or they had stopped him and now he was just standing there looking for some dirt side road. But the air in here! If you stay here, Alfred, you really will fall asleep. I jumped up, ran to the door, ran down the stairs and stopped outside. The clean, cold, slightly damp winter air allowed me to recover. Deep breaths, boy! Right, now my orders: a tractor?

Then something quite unexpected happened. From around the same corner I had passed just a few minutes earlier, six tired figures were walking together in single file. As the first one reached the stairs, he stumbled and looked up straight into my eyes. I looked down at him and saw that it was our Oberwachtmeister, the one who had led our three guns.

He was completely perplexed: 'Where did you come from, boy...?'

I was no less surprised: 'Herr Oberwachtmeister, where did *you* come from?!'

'We marched at night 30 kilometres behind the Russians,' he replied. 'Our vehicles ran out of fuel. Once we figured out where we were, we moved to the embankment next to the road. We marched on underlays and the Russians were 50 metres from us. As dawn began to break, we slid behind the embankment. We were lucky the road curved to the right and the embankment to the left, meaning we could separate ourselves from our "comrades" once more!'

'Yes, but there were eight of you. Where are the other two?'

'I couldn't get those two up. They were completely exhausted. I couldn't scream at them anymore. The "Ivans" were too close. Imagine that. An old soldier who can't scream anymore. What a shitty position! What's going on here?'

'This is the "Brandenburg" Regiment's command post. My gun is about 40 kilometres from here in a roadside ditch. I was supposed to find a tractor. The road to Poznań has been blocked by a T-34. The road to Hohensalza [Inowrocław] is still passable, I passed it about half an hour ago.'

'Take us there immediately, boy.'

A direct order! Sometimes there's something good about clear military relationships. I was relieved of the burden of acting on my own and, without another word, we set off.

As we marched through the park by the church, there was a sudden "boom!" as the first tank shell hit the roof with a great bang.

A StuG from the 1st Battery of the Assault Gun Battalion of the "Grossdeutschland" Division on the Eastern Front. In the middle is the then-commander of the 1st Battery, Oberleutnant Diddo Diddens, who was awarded the Knight's Cross.

We started to run. After 100 or 200 metres we ran out of breath. There was one final shot and we reached the exit road at a walking pace.

Outside the town, near its edge, we entered the open door of a butcher's shop. Obergefreiter Hans Ströcker[2] (an Austrian who I would later ride with in an assault gun during the fighting for Poznań, until he was injured), was a perfect "fixer". He disappeared for a few seconds before returning with a whole string of liverwurst slung around his neck. We then marched down the road, which was neither too long nor very wide. Behind us we could hear the sound of the engines: a column of trucks that had just found the last open exit road from the city.

Our Oberwachtmeister stuck out his thumb, but the first truck passed us without stopping. The second one did not, mainly because our Oberwachtmeister stepped out into the middle of the road with his machine gun loaded and aimed. His expression left the driver in no doubt. It was a bold move. We climbed onto the steps of the successive trucks, with the Oberwachtmeister getting on the last one.

We drove all day long. I could no longer say which way or how. The route led along main roads, minor roads, through groves, thickets, and meadows. Somewhere along the way we met a tired infantry soldier, who sat on the front left fender with the headlight between his legs. From time to time the drivers had to stop to follow the call of nature. When this happened, the soldier informed me that he had gone completely stiff and was in so much pain he could barely sit. So, we swapped places: me on the fender, he on the step. At one point I was alarmed by a kick or slap to my back. The driver had noticed I was swaying as if I was about to fall asleep. He would not really have cared if I had slipped to the left, but if I had accidentally slid under the front wheel, that would only add to our complications.

Somehow my infantryman friend found seats in the cab, wedged in between the driver and passenger. Hans Ströcker and I grinned at each other from one step to the other. At every turn, the liverwurst on the cab's roof shifted left and right, and each time we carefully moved it back to the centre.

Later, when it started to get dark, we reached a larger, stretched-out roadside village. It might have been Wreschen [Września], or maybe some other village. Stop, get off! With stiff legs, we shuffled off, one after another, and stared at each other. Nothing! At the very back of the column, one soldier broke off and approached us. It was Obergefreiter Ströcker, our gunner. As for the others? At some corner, part of the column had obviously turned right while we went left. They must have agreed to it. We never heard anything from them again. It was a shame – the Oberwachtmeister was a nice guy!

We went to a country house. The residents were just packing up, they wanted to escape. There was a half-full pot of coffee on the stove. The liquid was still warm and we could help ourselves – the hostess told us that we were not the first to do so. Malt coffee, meatloaf from a bread bag and thick slices of liverwurst on top. Satisfied, we discovered a pile of straw next to the stove and a kind of curtain above it. It looked like we were not the first ones here, either. We had clearly been overtaken while we were wondering what to do next.

Next morning, we got up at the crack of dawn. A deathly silence reigned everywhere. One of us went out to explore the area. An old Pole from a neighbouring house spoke to him in fairly decent German. He confirmed that the column of civilians had left the village around midnight. He had stayed. What could the Russians do to him? He was Polish. What would he do in Germany? He was right, and I hope fortune shone on him. And the column of trucks? Oh, they had stayed for maybe an hour.

After refuelling using the canisters, packed lunches were distributed and eaten. Some of the drivers changed places with their replacements and set off that evening. They did not care about us, of course. After all, who cares about passengers who pay their way by pointing submachine guns in your face?

HOW I BECAME A FIGHTER FOR POZNAŃ

There were still embers in the stove, under the ashes, so we could heat the coffee left in the pot. The rest of the bread and liverwurst was enough for our breakfast. Then we set off, on foot. The morning was cold, wet and foggy. The visibility was about 700-800 metres at best – and we were walking along the main road. We just needed to start singing: 'Three Japanese with a Double Bass…'. But instead of a double bass we had submachine guns. This lasted maybe half an hour, then we heard the sound of engines behind us. Listen! After a while, one of us said: 'That T-34 sounds a bit different!' We were very relieved. It is always good to have a professional with you. What emerged from the mist after some time was a three-wheeled delivery truck, which was very popular at that time: a flat bed at the back, a narrow cab at the front, a pointed bonnet with a single drive and guiding wheel. Above the wheel, on the swingarm of the front wheel, was the engine with the power of an Enten or Goggo, but it was still lively.

This time, we stood there with our thumbs out. In the cab were two well-wrapped up figures, looking at us. As the truck rolled past, the driver took his foot off the gas, pressed the clutch and stopped. We were taken on board. The elderly woman sitting inside probably thought that the three soldiers with guns were a military escort. She could not have known about our ridiculous stockpile of ammunition.

We sat in the back on a pallet, on some kind of thin tarpaulin, under which was a strange, hard, cold load. One of us eventually lifted the tarpaulin and found we were sitting on a dozen cleaned and frozen half pig carcasses. I sometimes think whether it was "our" butcher from Warthbrücken with his last liverwurst?

We got to Poznań quite quickly. On the outskirts of the town, we knocked on the roof of the cab, jumped down, and thanked the driver. He did not hang around too long. He must have made it to his destination, as the pig carcasses could easily be exchanged for gasoline, which he would no doubt have found out.

We marched along the fence of a long factory or barracks building, on the righthand side of the street. Poznań was considered a target and the place we were to regroup, should any of us be scattered somewhere along the way, which had happened to us. This was where the ultimate improbability happened! We had not even walked 50 metres when a passenger car, the well-known Kübelwagen, rolled past us down the street, towards the city. The person accompanying the driver gave us a strange look. I was already glancing instinctively at the car - we were a motorized unit after all - and suddenly yelled out: 'There, the one with the painted white helmet. He's from our division!' The white helmet (the so-called Stahlhelm) was the tactical sign of our division. All three of us started yelling: 'Hello, hey, stop…!' The car turned right, the passenger door opened, and the soldier turned towards us. We stood facing each other. It was Oberleutnant Hallmann, the commander of our brave unit from Kutno. A pause... and then: 'You guys have fallen from heaven! We've just unloaded a transport of eight howitzers for the brigade at the railway station. Each one with a two-man crew.[3] The 500th Assault Gun Training and Reserve Battalion is here, but they can't give us any men. I've been running around Poznań since yesterday evening in search of anyone who's heard a shot from a cannon at least once in their life.' One of us mumbled '...So we came just in time...' or something like that. What is perhaps most incredible about all this is that I have managed to keep this event in my memory.

Oberleutnant Hallmann invited us to his car and explained that the Prussians also had a full complement of men, but we could not have any. First, we had to go to the rendezvous point for survivors to register, then he could take us with him. The assembly point was on the right, behind the fence, and our ride was over after about 200 metres. We were met by the sentry, the Oberleutnant seemingly a well-known figure there. The Unteroffizier handed us over to his secretary and we were registered. We even received provisions and were able to lay down on the rotten floor inside the building. After all, a soldier must be able to sleep in all conditions, whether resting or in reserve. In the late afternoon we were picked up by a liaison officer, accompanied by our Oberleutnant. On the way to the car, the driver, an Obergefreiter, told us what it was going to be like getting us out of there. Telephone calls back and forth from the battery office in Kuhndorf (the Golęcin barracks in Poznań) to the unit commander, then to the local headquarters, next to the station headquarters, and to the rendezvous point for the survivors. Questions here and there to make sure everything was correct, whether the guns had actually been unloaded, whether the service was incomplete, whether the Prussians really could not hand over any men etc.[4] We were accepted by this hero immediately, but getting out of his clutches was a problem indeed. Today, I sometimes ask myself where those registration documents could have gone.

We went to our colleagues at the 500th Battalion's barracks in Golęcin. There were guns in the courtyard. The Obergefreiter led us to one of the barracks. The door was open and inside there was a cheerful noise and a great commotion. Sixteen brave men were

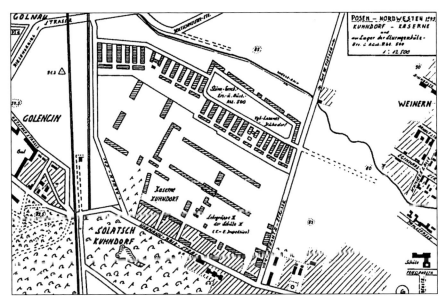

The location of the 500th Assault Gun Battalion's barracks in Golęcin, along with the adjacent barracks of the 5th Infantry Cadet School – the so-called Kuhndorf Camp.

sat there and were – I am sorry, but it was true - happily getting drunk. The explanation for this state of affairs was simple. One of the sixteen, my roommate, came from Magdeburg, where his father owned a vineyard. The son had contacted his father, and the father had then made contact with the transport manager, the Oberwachtmeister. Concerned about his son and the morale of his unit, the father had procured supplies from his vineyard for transportation. Three crates, each with twenty bottles of light or semi-dry Mosel wine, marked the beginning of this journey.

After unloading it in Poznań, it was considered that the first immediate need had arrived, and the first crate had been opened. Due to the lack of glasses, each man had received a bottle: sixteen men equalled sixteen bottles, plus us three equalled nineteen, plus the driver – the Obergefreiter - equalled twenty. And so the first crate was emptied. By the time we arrived, the bottles were already half empty, hence the encouragingly cheery welcome. Meanwhile, our Leutnant

The railway ramp at the former barracks of the 500th Assault Gun Training and Reserve Battalion (Kuhndorf Camp), as seen in 2001.

left without taking a drink. He was constantly travelling between ⊂ office and another anyway. The officers sometimes had a harder timᴇ than their subordinates.

I remember when, late in the evening, the door opened and the Oberleutnant stood there. 'Attention!' No reports or similar barrack behaviour was allowed. There was complete silence in the room as he informed us briefly and definitively: 'Men, the situation is not so much serious as hopeless. Poznań has been declared a fortress!'

'Not serious, but hopeless...' His subordinates enjoyed the wordplay, and the subsequent applause was deafening. Our officers knew how to talk to their men.

The next day, we had exactly twenty-four hours to prepare for this order. With us was a fusilier [Editor's note - this term was used in the Wehrmacht from about 1943/44], who had received his training at the Sturmgeschütz[5] school in Guben [Gubin] and had afterwards been drafted into the fusiliers [infantry accompanying the assault guns].

The former barracks of the 500th Assault Gun Training and Reserve Battalion in 2001.

ᵗᵉ

ʰadly wounded and burned in the casemates of the
was under the care of the medics.

ˡion gave ten men from its staff. The crews were
_...s fully fuelled and supplied with ammunition. The
ᴜnd pantry administrator were generous, having learned from
previous retreat situations. They took particular note of us ragged
survivors, who were wearing nothing but old uniforms. New and
warm underwear, new fur vests, new camouflage uniforms – if
requested – leather gloves (important when getting out of a burning
gun), everything was there. I have fond memories of the brand-new
high boots I received. On 23 February, a Pole took them off my feet
and gave me his old army boots for them. In all my life – sooner or
later – I have never seen shoes on human feet as damaged as those
Polish boots. The fear of water getting in the shoes was completely
unjustified because the holes in the sole let out twice as much water
as poured over the top. I wore them until my stay in the Petrosawodsk
camp in summer of 1945.

A German assault gun decorated for a ceremony at the barracks.

Much later, I started to think how senseless the occupation policy was, which forced the normal, basically inconspicuous and certainly not particularly important, but at the same time not necessarily hostile citizen of the occupied country, to wear such shoes in the winter before 1944/45. We were not surprised by most of the things that happened to us. But, as I said, these thoughts came later. Until 23 February 1945, I felt a hellish anger at the guy who took my shoes. You cannot expect too much from a 19-year-old!

Then, our seasoned "fixers" asserted their rights. We had a Kübelwagen, with which we began more earnest supply and requisition journeys. We used crates to haul black pudding and liverwurst from the supply warehouses. Then there were the gun crews that had to support themselves and their accompanying infantry all day long. Hans Ströcker, our aimer and a good mate from the gun, was one of the main drivers behind the evening plundering expeditions. Systematic searches were carried out in the abandoned, once "well-off", houses of fugitive German families, to find jars of food. They were professionally selected. Only strawberries and cherries were lugged into laundry baskets. Later, due to the lack of water, we quenched our thirst with the Mosel wine and strawberry and cherry compote. We ate them backwards: first we drank the entire contents of the jar, and then we spat out the cherry pips on the ground. The end. A righteous Russian might say today that we deserved twenty-five years for 'harming the Red Army by plundering its rightful spoils in advance!' In 1949, judgments with such or similar arguments were by no means uncommon.

It was still dark when, according to my calculations, the alarm was announced on 22 January 1945. Six guns, under command of Hauptmann Haller, headed to the east or southeast of the city. On the outskirts, the first contacts with the enemy were already taking place between the weak German security troops and the Russian reconnaissance troops. We escaped from there.

A postcard from the 500th Assault Gun Training and Reserve Battalion.

HOW I BECAME A FIGHTER FOR POZNAŃ

The German backup reports had to be more accurate than those of the Russians. Before noon, after a few hesitant movements back and forth, we stood so that a complete Russian infantry battalion in marching formation, and without any backup, came straight towards our well-concealed guns. The distance was about 400-600 metres, with smooth, frozen farmland on the left and right side of the road, when six of our guns simultaneously opened fire. From the second shot, the aimers only fired at a closer distance with a slightly delayed ignition – the "comrades" on the other side died in a shower of shrapnel, with no noteworthy resistance. About 150 shots (twenty-five from each of the six guns) were enough. Nothing moved on the other side until evening, when we were summoned to another location. The dance for Poznań would absorb us until the bitter end!

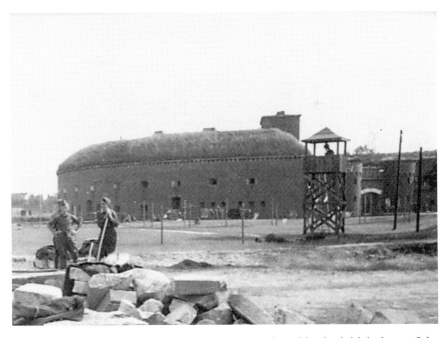

Fort Rauch, where Alfred Kriehn's crew was stationed in the initial phase of the battle for Poznań, together with several other crews of German armoured vehicles fighting in the eastern part of the Festung. This photograph was taken in 1940, when the fort was used to intern French prisoners of war.

Initially, we remained in the sector as a precaution due to our reduced number of guns. It was a very frequent and arduous task to act as backup at this stage of the war. If I remember correctly, our assault gun stood in an open field, slightly hidden by a row of houses which were occupied by our infantry.

Suddenly, there was a great deal of activity among us. One of us dug a long ditch in the field, while another arranged a few bricks and skilfully laid them on the sides. A sack of potatoes was pulled from one of the food crates, and one of the men pulled out some pans. When everyone realized what was happening, they got out their penknives and started peeling the potatoes. Meanwhile, peeled onions, fat, oil and salt were taken out from another corner of the crate. With a small adjustment to the nozzle, the soldier with the frying pan set the appropriate blast towards the flame of the kerosene lamp, and the "flamethrower" snorted as the potatoes fried in the pan. Raw potatoes could be baked or at other times stewed when the lid was put on, meaning you had half fries and half fried potatoes [Editor's note - this dish was considered a delicacy in the Rhineland before the war]. The smell hit our noses and as the frying pan circulated among us, suddenly, without any order, twelve people pulled out cutlery (a Wehrmacht essential!) from their trouser pockets, rather than use penknives. After all, a soldier lives by food! This was how a small camp was established. We had barely finished when a new order reached us and from that moment until the evening of 28 January1945, we stayed almost continuously in our assault gun, taking breaks only to refuel, replenish our ammunition and to stretch our legs.

At that time, our area of operation probably covered mainly the southern section of the city, including the wedge of the Russian attack from the south where they crossed the city and the River Warta, where they concentrated their attack. At the very beginning (far on the outskirts of the city) we came across an IS-2 Stalin tank. We almost missed it, and very nearly would have driven right over it. It was on an exit road from the city, near some detached buildings, with a small side street alongside. We turned right into it. At the same moment, Sepp shouted from behind his viewfinder: 'Stalin!' Unteroffizier Helmut Ebel also saw it from the turret hatch: 'Sepp, retreat!' At that moment, no one thought about saving the engine and gearbox. Sepp pulled back our cart - that's what we called our vehicle – turning blindly as the driver led him to the left, into the street we had just come from. The loader looked back to see if everything was alright. At that moment, a shell from the Stalin whizzed low in front of us. None of us had ever heard the sound of a 122-mm shell flying so close before. Armoured grenade fuses were set "hard", and this one could have settled as an unexploded shell after hitting the ground. There were probably many more tons of steel contained within its explosive charge as it lay there on the ground.

Meanwhile, Sepp steered the vehicle in reverse between two apartment blocks. We stood close to the wall, which protected us on the right. Our barrel barely protruded from around the corner as the shell was loaded. It was a fragmentation shell for 105-mm howitzer, as we had only received armour-piercing shells later. In fact, we were only given them from the end of 1944. Now the fun could begin. The fragmentation shell had a short range, and with a bit of luck, its impact could just about be stronger than a slight knock. But we had no choice.

At such moments, Sepp was very focused, while Hans kept his hands on the dials of his aiming device and was silent. We received the final orders from the driver's seat:

'Throw it in his tub, right under the turret. Maybe we'll get lucky and hit him under the turret's rotating rim. If the turret gets stuck, we'll have time to re-shoot.'

But nothing happened for a long time. Several minutes passed, no noises, nothing. Finally, Helmut, who had a background as an infantryman (necessary for an assault gun driver anyway) climbed out through his hatch and, half crawling, disappeared around the corner of the house to investigate the situation. He took quite a long time, but

Soviet IS-2 tanks from the 34th Heavy Tank Regiment on the streets of Poznań at the end of January 1945.

at last he came back and climbed up into the vehicle. As he lowered himself onto the seat he said 'He's gone. He's just disappeared. You can't see anything, guys. It's a miracle he escaped from us!'

Years later, I learned from reading publications on the use of assault guns that there was an order in the Red Army similar to that of our Führer's. According to this order, commanders were not to engage in combat with German assault guns if it could be avoided. Even the Russians, who were rather wasteful in terms of equipment, realized their losses were too high. Their commander must have known they had missed their target. Maybe the impression they made had been enough for him. One of the artillery rules was: 'If the shell hits, good. If not, its effect will still be electrifying.' The discussion ended with a statement that came from within the depths of the gun, somewhere to the left of the driver: 'Thinking about the whole incident and comparing their gun calibre to our armour, I don't think anything could have happened. The shell would just go through it like butter, in at the front, out the back, and then explode 5 metres away.' I don't know if it was cunning or Austrian slyness, but our driver was always cracking jokes. Everyone laughed whether they wanted to or not, believing that no one would voluntarily let their head be shot off.

I remember one sunny day when we were summoned to one of the streets leading out of the city. Unfortunately, I can no longer remember in what direction. The Russians were advancing very quickly along this street, right to the very centre of the city. Just before a road junction, a figure emerged from the shadows of the houses and, waving his arms, approached our gun from the side. The man warned us that one of our comrades had just been shot dead at the crossroads in front of us. Without knowing it, we would have driven directly into the T-34's field of fire, because we had no idea how deep the Russians had already penetrated. Post-war accounts of comrades-in-arms often described how far the information provided by the command forces of the Citadel deviated from what was actually happening on the front line, mainly due to the rapidly changing situation. In this case, we were probably facing a similar situation. Unfortunately, I do not remember which member of our assault gun crew was hit at that time. But, if my memory serves me right, I managed to save several other members, and the Russian advance was temporarily halted by our presence there. We took up positions in such a way that we had an open space and connecting streets within our field of fire. On the other side, under the cover of houses, the T-34 was lurking. We were both aware of each other's presence, so we tried not to leave our hideout under any circumstances during the day. The first one who did so would be finished. I am not sure, but I think that was when my machine gun failed me.

At this point, let me make a small digression regarding our weapons and assault gun (Sturmgeschütz). Overall, it was a great weapon due to its low construction resulting from the lack of a turret. It was also well camouflaged in the field. When the gun was facing the enemy, it showed its best armoured part. The narrow silhouette was directed towards the enemy. Our Sturmgeschütz, however, also had weaknesses. For example, the space inside the vehicle was so limited that there was not enough room for five crew members and a built-in machine gun, such as in the Panzer III tank. This meant that when fighting in close range with enemy infantry hiding in their foxholes, we had to be accompanied by our own infantry to protect us. Another solution was simply to ensure maximum vigilance during fierce, close combat with the enemy. The only help was the machine gun, which was mounted on top, in front of the loader's hatch. This solution, however, only worked at longer distances because the loader protruded halfway out of the hatch, thus risking becoming a target himself. In addition, there was also a shield folded in front of the loader's hatch, where the machine gun was mounted. The loader fired from behind the shield, which provided cover from enemy infantry fire. The guns we had at our disposal in Poznań in 1945 were slightly better equipped. The machine gun was loosely mounted and was operated and aimed from inside using an angle mirror and sights (aiming devices). To do this, the shooter would hold something that resembled a bicycle handlebar, if I may use that comparison, which allowed him to turn the machine gun. Meanwhile, the trigger was operated by a handle on the right, similar to a handbrake. The connection to the weapon ran above, over the shooter and through the floor pull.

Our assault guns were transported in winter on rail wagons, before being unloaded and set off for action. There was snow, then there was a thaw, then frost again, and it probably rained a bit, too. The crews got on and off continuously, so to put it bluntly, it was always dirty. Individual parts had been oiled previously, but when? One day, I wanted to fire but for some reason the trigger was suspiciously hard to pull. Oh well. All of a sudden, there was a slight release, but the gun still did not fire. I looked around and suddenly noticed that the floor tension cable had been torn from its bracket, probably due to the freezing water. The welded seam put in place was not exactly what we would have called "German efficiency", but oh well. It was like that for several days as we had no time to stop by the mechanics or the repair department. Finally, I tied a thick cord at the top of the gun's trigger, took the free end between my teeth, and aimed with my hands. It worked! I just had to be careful not to break the gun.

Once, when the Russians managed to get quite far towards the city centre, we were standing at the command post of another section. Suddenly, the commander drew our attention to the fact that the wide, beautiful steps not far from us were the steps leading to the Poznań Opera House. There was even a park around us. I remember waiting for our gun commander and checking the line in the lagging of my blocked floor tension cord. There was always time to deal with such things during those kinds of breaks, even though the fighting companies were only a few streets away. It was strange to think that until recently, smartly dressed people had gone up those stairs to relax and take part in their cultural heritage, despite the war. How did it that fit in with the current situation and my dirty hands? There would be other moments of confusing calm during those early days.

I also remember a morning we spent along one of the railway lines leading out of the city. The scenery had something of the atmosphere of a freight station. There were railway tracks, crossroads, barns, and a barracks a little further away. The sun barely broke through the clouds and there was not much going on. The driver of our gun, as usual, set out on foot on a reconnaissance to find out what the situation ahead of us was like. No one in the rear was able to give us such information. German soldiers were nowhere to be seen, so who knew where they were? Every now and then, a shadow dressed in civilian clothing slipped from one barrack to another. Was it someone in search of loot? It was very quiet. I sat on the top of the gun, my legs dangling down into the hatch. I was holding an almost empty jar in my hand with cherries inside. I happily ate the rest of the jar, spitting the seeds left and right as I wished. Some brave housewife had boiled them and selected just the right amount of sugar. The cherries were delicious; I still remember them to this day.

Nothing special happened around us, except that they finally called us out of there. But there were also other situations, such as one night, in the first days of fighting, when we were called to support a strong counterattack by the "Lenzer" Battle Group. I remember that evening, the darkness and the wide tree-lined avenue. Lenzer's men had to defeat the enemy, and we provided them with covering fire. We shot at the houses across the street where the Russians had taken up position. Then the Lenzer soldiers crossed the wide avenue in one leap with characteristic determination. The Russians fled in panic and left behind what they had lugged with them a long way: light and heavy anti-tank guns and light anti-aircraft guns. They often reacted like that during street fights. According to reports, our men blew up a heavy howitzer in one of the yards.

HOW I BECAME A FIGHTER FOR POZNAŃ

The break took place when a T-34 tank spotted us and tried to sneak sideways between the trees. We heard a suspicious sound and Helmut recognised it in advance. He set the gun's range to 150 metres, if I remember correctly. We already had something completely new for us on board: armour-piercing shells for a 105-mm howitzer. Until now, howitzers only fired fragmentation ammunition. Meanwhile, looking through the peephole, Sepp became very angry: 'Hans, he's turning the turret!' Hans mumbled something like, 'I've got it…!' And then to me: 'Ready?'

'Ready!'

He put his finger on the trigger and said 'Fire!' The sound of the shot was such that I looked at the gun breech as it moved backwards and thought: 'Just a few more centimetres and I'll be stuck in the wall between the combat and engine compartments.'

Hans had his eyes at the optics again: 'What do you think, Helmut? Give him one more to finally light up?' But Unteroffizier Ebel, with his eyes at the binoculars, said: 'Leave him, he's had enough. Fragment shell'. This final action was aimed at me, and the wall opposite received even more holes. For this action, the crew was awarded the Iron Cross 1st Class (EK I), with the exception of the loader. When Hauptmann Haller noticed, as he put the ribbon in my buttonhole, that I did not yet have the Iron Cross 2nd Class (EK II), and seeing the empty space on my chest, he said to me: 'You'll complete the set another time.'

'Yes, Herr Hauptmann!' I said, with my upright posture and stern face, as was customary. In any case, the tank in the street was apparently unusable in some way, as it stood nearby with its barrel hanging at an odd angle.

A few days later, as we were sitting together eating, Hans said something that made us think: 'Just think, these houses we're firing at will all have to be rebuilt later! It'll be a lot of work!' None of us had ever thought that the houses we were shooting at had been and were supposed to be houses and flats again after the war. A flat? What was that? And when will we see one again?

We all genuinely laughed at Hans' statement: 'That'll be a lot of work!' He was probably the only one of us who did not survive the battles for Poznań. He was injured right at the very end, when everything from anesthetics to simple injections was in short supply.

I must digress a little again here to prove that I had the right to mix up some of the events of those first days.

At that time, it was normal for us, i.e. assault gun crews located on the outskirts of the city, to be delivered a warm meal from the Citadel. So our vehicle carrying the supplies drove around Poznań, with another person from the kitchen sat next to the driver, holding the pots. One day we did not receive anything, and in the evening we returned to the Citadel to replenish our almost completely used ammunition and to refuel. Our commander, seeing that we could cope without him, went to the kitchen to explain the situation. He must have been very hungry, too. The Unteroffizier chef listened to him calmly, then replied that it was not his or his kitchen's fault. His driver had chased us around the city for about two hours. When he got to the third place of action and heard again that we had missed each other because we had left fifteen minutes earlier, and no one knew where we had gone to, he thought that the soup was already cold and we would have to come back for ammunition anyway. Therefore he was more likely to meet us at the Citadel. And he was right as we arrived about half an hour after him.

How can anyone think I can remember all the action we witnessed? There is, however, one case I remember vividly, which involved the counter-attack of the Fahnenjunkers (cadets of the cadet school) late in the evening of 27 January 1945, and was carried out towards the railway embankment leading from Dębiec to Starołęka. We took part in this action at night, and knew nothing about what had happened there during the day. We waited by one of the old forts near the River Warta, and I remember sitting in one of the dank casemates when our commander was summoned to receive new orders.

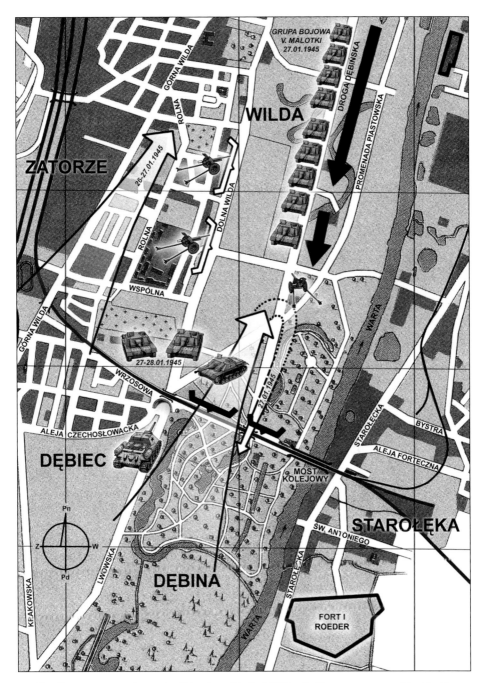

The German counter attack of the "von Malotki" Battle Group, supported by StuGs, fighting in the Dębiec area on 27-28 January 1945.

I also remember something else very well from that time. When we were driving our gun, Hans or Sepp would often call out to me: 'Alfred, open the bottle!' I would then open a bottle of Mosel wine from our provisions chest (the bottle opener was essential, you cannot die of thirst in the desert with a full bottle!). I would take a test sip. We did it so that the commander was served first, then the bottle would circulate and reach me empty, as I was the last one. That is why I took a test sip first. However, one evening I had a little suprise. What I felt in my throat was not quite a liquid. It was so cold, like a mixture of wine and ice, but was quite pleasant even so. Nevertheless, I had heard that frozen high-proof alcohol can be dangerous as a man burns so many calories during its digestion that it can be poisonous for the throat and stomach. But everyone was OK so the Mosel wine was probably low percentage.

The action took place that night with nine assault guns. We were the fifth in the column. Our way of providing support must have been strange for the Fahnenjunkers. The ground for attack must have been 5 metres across, or even a little less. On our left was the River Warta, while on the right were buildings. Our tanks avoided the wetland forests along the river like the plague because they were very swampy and an armoured vehicle could be halted there very quickly. On the right, the Fahnenjunkers advanced in an expanded formation. It was very easy to run over your own men in the dim light, so the guns rode carefully, one after the other, with only the first in the column firing and the rest simply following behind.

From the morning of 22 January we had neither action nor a break. I was awake when the counter-attack began, then I fell asleep near the ammunition. I slept through the attack for a good 1.5 kilometres, until the railway crossing at Dębiec. There, the infantry came under fire from Russian mortars. I woke up to the unpleasant sound of explosions, and was completely awake when our commander shouted: 'Helmut, close the hatch, I don't want shrapnel in my vehicle!' We passed under the railway tracks, which could only be a crossing at the intersection of Dolna Wilda and Piastowska streets on the northern side of the railway line (Dolna Wilda Street extends to the southside).

Around midnight, the Fahnenjunkers fought with the Russians in the dense buildings of Dębiec. At that time, we provided backup on the left flank towards the southern part of the Dębina forest. Our gunner screamed when he got a hit: 'Got him!' The target was a truck towing an anti-tank gun. The Fahnenjunkers were then ordered to withdraw, as any further night action was impossible. They were ordered to fall back behind the railway line, where a fighting position was created the next day. I still remember whistling and shouting: 'Everything's collapsed over there!'

Some 60-70 metres in front of me was a lighthouse, which, by some miracle, was still burning. It would not matter if, at some point, a figure emerged from the shadows and crossed the street. It would disappear into the darkness on the left and was probably just some sleepy Russian. My machine gun was not loaded. We had no ammunition and the tapes hung and got in the way by the hatch. In addition, this all happened at night, when there were usually no particular targets. However, I immediately remembered that we were at war. I grabbed my submachine gun, but it would not work. All I heard was the slow strike of the firing pin on the shell. It needed to be reloaded. With one movement, a full cartridge fell out and the next went into the barrel. By now, the Russian has long since disappeared. I pulled the trigger again and history repeated itself. It was the effect of all that frost and dirt.

In the morning, we stood behind the railway embankment, with the infantry on top of it. The command staff decided that nine guns at this location were too many, so we were informed that six should return to the Citadel for new orders. Our commander was slowly returning, with the others rushed. 'We're staying here!' he said, and to me, 'Tell me, how many more rounds do we have?'

'Six rounds!'

He eyes widened: 'How many?!'

'Six!'

He jumped out, but there was nothing more to be done. The others had already left. Oh well!

I do not know if I remember the sequence of the morning events correctly, but before noon there were suddenly 10-15 minutes of shelling, but to no avail. It was just the fire of anti-tank guns and tanks. Their flat-flying projectiles either hit the railway embankment or flew away. There were infantry with mortars on the railway embankment and to hit them you had to aim exactly at the crest of the embankment. But they remained unhit. We got out of our vehicle. A hit to the roof itself was rather unlikely. There was silence, then suddenly the sound of tank engines. We received reports that two Russian armoured guns armed with 122-mm weapons were heading towards the underpass. We stood in a semicircle: a 75-mm gun, our 105-mm howitzers, and a third StuG with a short barrel called 'Stummel'.

I remember asking one of the others at the embankment: 'Does anyone else have any armour-piercing rounds?' They all shook their heads. No one had any left. The projectile was in the barrel, range about 50 metres. At least it would knock it out when it hit. Fully focused, Sepp said: 'Hans, aim to the side, straight around the drive wheel. If you manage to drop a caterpillar on it, at least it'll be immobilised.' Hans nodded. The infantrymen, of course, were listening to what we were saying. They did not like it because the shrapnel from these three shells might hurt them, as they were laying next to and on top of the embankment.

While we were waiting for the first enemy, an infantry soldier armed with a Panzerfaust suddenly approached from the right. He lay down to our left, at the very edge of the sloping bank. So we had a break. Twelve pairs of eyes observed the embankment intently as we waited to see what would happen. The noise was getting louder, the tunnel rumbled louder and louder, and this guy was just lying there, quite close. A shot, a flash from the muzzle, and in front of it, like a tennis ball, a small but ever faster Panzerfaust warhead. Inside the tunnel we heard an angry sound and saw a cloud of smoke coming out of it. The shooter got up, brushed the dust off, and after a while, holding only the barrel in his hand, went back to where he had come from. He looked at us as if to say: 'You armoured men always have the wrong ammo when you're needed!' And he was right.

We went down to assess the situation. The Russian self-propelled gun stood there, immobile and completely silent. There was just enough room to its left and right for one man to squeeze through. Behind the gun, in the southern part of the Dębina forest, about 70-80 metres away, we saw the second gun retreating in reverse gear. It was unable to fire because of its comrade. Due to the lack of space, we were also unable to fire back at him, and it was too far away for the infantry on the embankment, as well.

We looked ominously at each other. Someone said that the Panzerfaust does not destroy by shrapnel alone, but by the pressure

The road underneath the Dębiec-Starołęka railway line in 2006. Here, on the morning of 28 January 1945 (in a tunnel that no longer exists), a German soldier destroyed a Russian self-propelled gun with a Panzerfaust.

inside the enemy armoured vehicle. We listened to this explanation in passing as we stood next to the lifeless giant. The dead crew sat inside, thier eardrums and lungs ruptured, blinded by the explosion. What fascinated us most was the tiny hole in the front armour that the Panzerfaust had burned through. The hole was maybe 45-50 mm in diameter and had smoothly burned through all the layers of armour, or at least that is how it looked. The Panzerfaust was a weapon we knew about but did not use. We had a machine-versus-machine war, where we were just the operators.

That morning, we received information that all six assault guns that had been withdrawn had been hit over a distance of 1.5-2 kilometres. The weather was foggy and unclear. The mist absorbed all sound, but I was surprised that there was no noise behind us. After all, loud shots from anti-tank guns or tanks were impossible not to hear 1 kilometre away, or maybe even a little more. Maybe the Russians had something similar to our Panzerschreck or the American bazooka at their disposal?

Our commanders looked worried, as our right flank was practically exposed. We had to turn back after dusk at the latest and could not manage another day without any ammunition. In such moments, our driver Sepp behaved sensationally: 'Don't be afraid, I can do it. If I drive at 60 kilometres an hour without the clutch, in second gear, no one will hear us for 50 metres.' And he was not showing off; he actaully did it. He released the brakes so gently they did not even squeak, let alone the tracks. The three Sturmgeschütze rode off in complete darkness, maintaining a good distance.

The commander and loader leaned halfway out of the hatches, listening to the darkness for any signs of an enemy gun. But nothing happened. From time to time we passed the looming silhouettes of our comrades' guns. Some had gone to hell the day before.

The day passed relatively calmly, although at one point the commander barked at me. It was also part of the loader's job to prepare cold provisions when, as now, we were at a safe distance

A Sturmgeschütz III Ausf. G destroyed in the morning of 28 January 1945 at the intersection of Piastowska Street (Grillparzer Weg, Skagerrak Allee) and Droga Dębińska (Eichwaldstr.). The vehicle's name, given by its crew, is visible on the gun barrel: Trudl.

from the line. So I cut the bread, opened the 850g can of sausage, cut thick slices and served it all to my hungry friends. A hungry infantryman saw what I was doing and approached me as I sat on the engine cover, asking if he could also have something. I gave him a thick sandwich, an even thicker piece of sausage, and an extra slice of bread. He thanked me and left happily. 'Why didn't you just give him the whole can?!' I hadn't expected that, but at least the soldier went away satisfied. Better to shut up in such cases. At night we helped with the refuelling and replenishment of the ammunition at the Citadel. We ate almost nothing, before laying down near the Citadel barracks on a prepared bed of straw. There was no point in speaking to us for the next twenty-four hours.

The next evening we replaced another returning crew. Later, we often fought in the north of the city, initially on the northern side of the Zeppelinwiese,[6] in the vicinity of Golęcin, Winiar, and Piątkowo, but I am unable to be more precise.

The Zeppelinwise (airfield) in the northern part of the city.

I remember very clearly the action that took place at the end of January at the Citadel's North Gate. We stood there with ten guns fuelled and loaded. Each had two 200-litre drums of fuel loaded in the back, providing a total of 400 litres of reserve fuel! We were supposed to break through to the west, because a counter-attack from that direction, in the area of Bentschen [Zbąszyń], had been launched, which was intended to unblock Poznań. We were accompanied by Junkers from the 5th Cadet School. During the day we received word that the attack had been cancelled, and that the spare fuel drums were to be unloaded. Maybe that was for the best because the Russian infantry often fought with mortar support instead of machine guns (those guns also had less ammunition than our infantry) and we were not sure what would happen to the fuel drums loaded on our vehicles. The commanders just said we were to refuel as soon as possible and to get rid of them, which was necessary since we were not going to break through.

I do not know much about the actions that took place in the north of Poznań, but some miracles happened there. We smashed a few fences driving around the backyards and hanging around the corners of the houses. Mesh fences consist of fairly solid wire, and many metres of them became tangled in the caterpillars, which slowed down the vehicles more and more. One afternoon, we were stood with three guns at the Zeppelinwiese airfield and, with hammers, pliers and wire cutters, we removed the wire caught in the tracks. It was painstaking work. There were three men at the gun and a driver looking out of the hatch or inside the gun. The instructions were as follows: a metre forward, back a little bit etc.

The same was happening in the StuG next to us. The gun commander was kneeling on the ground, giving the driver's commands, while the other two crew members were pulling... but nothing happened. Eventually, one of them climbed onto the gun and saw the dead driver in his seat. He had been shot in the head! At the time I thought it was a stray bullet, but today I think it must have been a well-aimed shot from some Pole in a nearby house. The Poles were generally peaceful, but they were certainly not our allies, and weapons were widely available.

The crew buried their driver by the beautiful old trees on the north side of the Citadel. The park area used to be the mound of the Citadel, and we stayed there a lot during the final days of fighting as it provided cover from the aeroplanes. When I went back to the city in 1977, I could not find the exact tree again, despite the fact that we had passed it so often before.

There was one time when we had a good night's sleep in that area. The night was calm, and we had excellent infantry ahead of us. We parked the guns next to a two-story villa, and while one of us was on guard, the other three went into the building. We slept in the bedroom of the former residents who had fled. Two of us in a double bed and one on a mattress on the floor. It was amazing. In the morning, we went straight over to our infantry.

Later, it occurred to one of us that they had left something behind, so I was sent back. The room looked seemingly intact, but somehow different. It was kind of cold inside, and there was a coating of dust on everything. Next to one of the nightstands, slightly above the floor, was a large hole in the wall, about a metre in diameter and easy to walk through. The question was how had it suddenly appeared? We had spent the night there a few hours before, with the gun parked outside next to the entrance.

I still remember the night of 4 or 5 February. We had spent the day on the south side of the Zeppelinwiese, and it was time to pack up and head back to the Citadel. We made a large arc around the airfield in the dark, but there was something going on in the distance and we could see a dim light ahead. One or two more Ju-52s[7] landed and ambulances with red crosses and dim trunk lights appeared. I learned later that it was one of the last nights when the wounded and the Red Cross sisters were evacuated from the city. Later, as we sat on our hay in the Citadel and ate our food, one of us grumbled at how stupid we had been. We could easily have gone from our vehicle to the Ju-52. I wondered what people on the other side of the Oder would say? We began to think about the consequences of our actions. Somehow, I knew I had to get out.

At the end of January, we had found out that our Oberleutnant had fallen ill with diphtheria and was laid up in one of the casemates. One night, when I went to get a hot meal for us, the other three members of our crew went to visit him. They came back silent; he was not very well and there was no treatment for diphtheria there on the ground. About eight to ten days later, already well into February, we were woken up by the nurses. They told us that our commander was dead and that we should take care of his burial because they could not manage it. It was a funeral worth remembering. It took place a bit off the beaten track from our access road to the dilapidated façade of the main building. Shortly ahead us, another crew was buring their colleague. We started digging, but the top layer of earth was frozen. To the south, east and west, there was only very limited land still in our hands. Only to the north was there a little more of it. The Citadel was a large built-up area, and there was always something going on on its outskirts.

Suddenly, a Russian biplane flew over our heads. Heavily armoured, it looked like a relict from the First World War. Infantrymen who had been on the Eastern Front already knew it well, especially during its night-time operations. Our comrades-in-arms mentioned something about the fact that phosphorus (incendiary) bombs were dropped from this type of aircraft. Anyway, it soon became light again, and somewhere above us a glowing band shone like the aurora borealis, very low on the horizon. I really enjoyed those icy "Karelian" nights. Here, however, everytime it happened it meant a leap into the bushes. Our Oberleutnant now found himself on his own during this amazing spectacle, while we managed to dig our own knee-deep foxholes. We eventaully buried our Oberleutnant in the ground and while the Russians did not exactly salute him, at least they took care of the proper lighting for the ceremony. Two hours later and we were back laying on our hay. Four people were eventually buried in that place. Three from the Sturmgeschütz crews and a Luftwaffe pilot from an anti-aircraft battery. We did the best we could in the circumstances, and all four of them received crosses on their graves.

Sometime in mid-February, twin-engined Soviet bombers bombed the Citadel. At that time, we often provided backup by standing hidden among the trees in front of the Citadel's northern embankment, near the Tiger. I still remember very clearly those beautiful sunny days with blue skies before spring arrived. Then the enemy planes would fly over our heads at an altitude of about 1,500-2,000 metres - too high for our 20-mm anti-aircraft guns. A heavy anti-aircraft gun lay wrecked somewhere by the crossroads. The planes descended as if over a training field and then dropped their payload. Their bombs seemed to be as long as the plane itself, and most of them landed somewhere in the southern part of the Citadel. They did not detonate immediately, perhaps after ten or fifteen seconds had passed...these were time bombs. A moment later there would be a huge explosion, as waves of detonations passed under our feet. Our 26-ton spring-loaded vehicle worked like a seismograph. We look at each other in silence. Next to the headquarters of the fortress lay several combat troops, and there were hundreds of wounded in the casemates. Apparently we were not a sufficiently worthwhile destination for those at the top.

Several recurring events took place during our backup operation, and every single civilian will listen to this in disbelief. Early on, Hans had found a gramophone during one of his rides. It was very modern for the time, not just some old piece of junk with a big speaker. Of course, he did not have a needle, but Hans had thought of everything. He had a box of needles and a record collection, so when we were bored, someone always asked, 'Alfred, will you play the record?' So off I would go. Hans had built up quite a collection and they were all neatly arranged in a suitcase. We even had a playlist of

The ruins of the Citadel, 1945.

favourites, which were usually well-known songs like 'Lass mich heut Nacht nicht allein' (Don't Leave Me at Night) or from another album 'Chinamann liebt das Chinamädchen Marzipan' (A Chinese Man Loves a Chinese Girl called Marzipan). But whether it was China or Japan, it was certainly a long way from where we were. Colleagues who did not know either Puccini or Butterfly sang the chorus 'Marzipan'. Another song was 'Unter Der Rote Laterne von St Pauli' (Under the Red Lantern of St Pauli). None of us had ever been to Hamburg [Editor's note – St Pauli is the red-light distrcit of Hamburg], and now the city lay in ruins, but there was something captivating about the song.

Once, sometime during the fighting in the city, we were ordered to secure a factory yard. Out on the street, many people were queuing up for what seemed to be the last source of water in the city. Suddenly, about 150-200 metres away, there was an explosion thanks to shelling from one of "Stalin's Organs".[8] It was not a problem for us because we were stood between tall buildings, but after that moment, our gramophone stopped working.

Later, a territorial protection soldier (Landesschützen), many of whom were in Poznań, appeared next to me. We never really had anything to do with them because they mainly dealt with the protection of warehouses, depots and railway lines.

'Are they going already? When will they be here? How much do they have left? You have a radio in your vehicle, what do they say?'

My face must have been blank, but he kept asking more and more questions. I failed to convince him that it was impossible. Our radio was useless between those tall buildings and completely unsuitable for receiving German broadcasts from the village of Königswusterhausen. The guy had thought our scratching needle was a transmitter. He finally went quiet and then left, disappointed that he had not received the news he wanted, especially from people who were considered privileged, in a way, since our armour at least protected us from infantry weapons.

Many years later, at the turn of the 1950s and 1960s, and already in the days of transistors and electronics, I heard an emotional comment from a someone about the increasingly popular pocket radios with large headphones. He spoke indignantly that one day, American infantrymen would go into battle with a cheerful blues in their ears. Then I thought to myself: 'You should've been there fifteen years ago, mate!' We almost missed a Russian missile hitting our roof, just as some sweet voice was singing 'I can't exist without your love...' Death usually comes to a soldier when he least expects it.

It was now the middle of February and it was becoming increasingly clear that the situation was hopeless. The garrison in the eastern part of the city had broken out to the north because the bridges had been destroyed and their location had become critical. It was rumoured that the Lenzers had broken out westward, against orders. On one morning, some crews returned to the Citadel because two other crews had tried their luck west, while they were sleeping. In such a situation, a message was sent to intercept them before they reached the Oder.

We were still going in circles between action, readiness and change. One night we were standing in front of the guardhouse of the Citadel's North Gate and the commander was reporting to the guard (just like in the barracks). A squad of tank destroyers might be lurking somewhere in case the T-34 tried to sneak past unexpectedly.

Suddenly, a line of soldiers from inside the Citadel silenty appeared, almost like shadows, and pushed past the gun. One of us recognized a familiar face. 'Yes, it's us. There are sixteen of us, eight are from our assault guns and the rest are SS. We've got special orders, which, if we complete, will allow us to break out to the west, depending on the situation and our own assessment.' Next to me stood my comrade-in-arms from Magdeburg, the one from the vineyard. He had a strange pale yellow face and slanted eyes, it was our Harry. I had always thought he looked rather Monglain in appearance. But we wanted to know more.

The bridge at the Citadel's North Gate, where groups of German soldiers tried to escape the surrounded fortress at various stages during the fighting.

'Take the equipment and move on,' said the squad leader, who left the guardhouse. The commander of our gun said: 'Get in, come on, come on, we can get in!' They disappeared into the darkness.

Many years later, I received a letter from Hanover. Harry's father, now an elderly man, had been allowed to go west and the German Red Cross had given him my contact details so that he could ask me about his son. He had received a final letter from him from Poznań, and the German Red Cross had reported that I had been there too. I wrote and told him everything I knew. He had even included a self-addressed and stamped return envelope, plus a strange request in that I was to return his original letter back to him. I thought about it for a long time, until finally a Red Cross representative explained to me that because I lived in the Soviet zone, doing this would be illegal and punishable by twenty-five years in prison. Harry's father was from Magdeburg and knew it would have been better for his letter not to fall into the wrong hands.

In the summer of 1977, I spent four weeks travelling through Poland. On the second day of the trip, passing through Frankfurt (Oder), I reached Poznań and the Citadel. By then there were no ruins anymore, but instead there was a "Friendship and Brotherhood" park, or something like that.[9] On the street that runs behind the Citadel, there were still many holes in the façades of houses where Richard Siegert's Tiger once stood. They were the result of infantry weapons and machine guns. My two sons wanted to photograph them, but I expressed my concerns about the reaction of the locals. On the other hand, my wife, who was also with me, wanted to admire and probably smell every rose that grew there. I was also concerned about my itinery and the plans for my visit. I did not visit the museum dedicated to the battles for Poznań, located in the southern part of the old fortifications. The "mandatory" T-34 was stood there on a concrete platform. I tried to orientate myself, but it was difficult. I entered from the north, under the shade of the old trees in front of the North Gate, slightly downhill, turned left along the path parallel to the embankment, then suddenly a sharp turn to the right. There was a break in the embankment and a large hole. Surprised, I stopped. Where had that hole come from? Where was I? Suddenly it dawned on me. I was at the old guardhouse at the North Gate. How many times had I come in and out of this way?

Memories suddenly came flooding back, even though it was around 14.00 on a beautiful July afternoon. I saw the shadows of those sixteen comrades in front of me. Yes...permission to break through... But it was impossible! I squeezed my eyes shut in disbelief, then stared at the remains of a wall, a wooden box, with a damp, cold, musty draft wafting from the crack. My God, it was a fragment of the casemate where we had gathered on the evening of 22 February 1945, just before the breakout. More on that later...

I realized where I was. Many later reports from Poznań describe the Russian breakthrough from the west towards the residential districts between the northern rampart of the Citadel and the Zeppelinwiese, which took place from 15-18 February. It was in that area that we achieved our final success, at the moment when the Russians were just about to head south. We had left some guns there, with the crews stood in some basement company command post, and the commander liaising with the company commander. A communication interrupted our conversation to say that one of our men had just been killed. Unteroffizier Ernst(?), a thin, blond man from Mecklenburg or Pomerania, had been hit in the head by a volley of mortar grenades. His skull and brain were shattered, but his face was still intact. His crewmates buried him in the Citadel, next to our Oberleutnant. They told us they had warned him about going outside, but he had been fidgety all afternoon.

The four of us were sitting in the basement when suddenly a company commander took our Unteroffizier aside. His Fahnenjunkers were on lookout and had seen that a company-strong Russian assault force had penetrated the apartment block near our position. Experience told us that the attack would come at dawn, when our infantry was still asleep. 'Isn't this something we can deal with?' Helmut said to Sepp, 'We'll have to be sneaky!' The three of us, Helmut outside the gun with the company commander and his squad, drove around the residential houses, through the gardens, far from the intersections and streets. From time to time our Unteroffizier positioned himself by the gun and gave us some tips, while behind him, Sepp gently turned the engine over. At the last corner, the Sturmgeschütz emerged and extended the barrel towards the dark, left-hand side of the apartment block ahead. The shell was already in the barrel, and the distance was 50-60 metres. This was to be the goal of our mission.

'Ready?'

'Ready!'

Finger on the trigger.

'Fire!' Hans commanded.

That night we rode around with a shell in the barrel and the breech locked, so we were ready to fire at any moment. Loading the next round took a matter of seconds, each time I would flick the key (which hung around my neck) and put the round into the chamber. 'Ready? Ready! Fire!' One by one. Sepp had only experienced the howitzer so far and could not get enough of it. I felt warm when he said, 'Such a succession of shots, it's amazing!' Suddenly, a scream came from outside. There was no need to be silent anymore.

'Take the wagon and turn right, now get the other half of the house!'

It was Helmut's voice! Sepp put his foot down and we drove 30 metres towards the hous. Once again: 'Ready? Ready! Fire!' Hans swung the barrel right, up, down, left, and back again. They must have fallen asleep!

'Enough!' shouted someone from outside. I had a lot of work emptying the empty shells out of the bag. I looked outside. The hits were not very obvious, but the windows looked strangely empty. Some gray rags were fluttering about. And the roof, where had the roof gone? Beams were jutting upward, silhouetted against the grey sky. We heard rustling. There was smoke and the smell of burning.

'Sepp, back up!' We heard an order from the darkness. 'You're standing there like you're on a platter!' Sepp retreated 20-30 metres into the darkness that protected us. Some figures appeared near the vehicle.

'Hans, get out, we'll take a closer look!'

Together with the company commander at the head, they disappeared. They returned after a while, and Hans commented: 'It looks good, there are a few, five, maybe eight in the stairwell, at the entrance to the basement, in the corridors. Half of one of them is stuck to the ceiling.' The attack did not happen the next morning. In fact, nothing interesting happened there.

I do not really remember the groups with loudspeakers that were supposed to weaken our morale. They proclaimed: 'Comrades, come to the other side, otherwise you'll all be destroyed!' They announced it in a grim voice, but we knew they wanted to annihilate us. Nothing was said about the 1,000 beautiful women supposedly waiting for us. Meanwhile, the food porters had reached the basement, but the dishes were to be returned to the Citadel kitchens as soon as possible. Some smartass had set up a zinc tub, cleaned it with snow, and now a home-made soup was swirling inside it. 'Join me!' said the Leutnant, waving his invitation to sit down. 'I always order supplies for ten more men than I actually have.'

Indeed, the infantry always treated us well when they had plenty of food. We sat down and started eating. It was one of the best soups I had ever tasted. Years later, when I told this story to one of my students, I knew what he would say.

'Don't you know that zinc is poisonous?'

'Yes,' I replied with a dismissive gesture. 'I know the story.' The story he had in mind was how, one Sunday in Swabia, there had been a party serving potato salad. With nowhere to store them, some unlucky chap came up with the idea of storing them in a zinc tub, where they were left until the day of the party. The end of the story is that twenty-one guests spent the night in the hospital and the rest healed themselves by vomiting everything up.

The time came when it was my friend Hans' turn. We were in the Citadel and entered Rawelin III, right in the eastern part of the Citadel, parallel to the embankment, on Szelągowska Street. In the east, the River Warta flowed north. The Russians were on the eastern bank, while our infantry, in turn, were on the embankment. We were not exactly quiet, but the Citadel was our home after all! Helmut disappeared into one of the casemates, as he always did, and Hans and I sat by the hatch and dangled our legs. I think we must have been heard on the other side, and the Russians finally had a detailed plan of the Citadel, because as we were talking, a volley of mortar grenades suddenly landed in front of our gun. We jumped back inside. I pulled myself together and heard Hans screaming, 'I'm hit!' He had a small cut under his eye, the size of a fingernail. Sepp crawled out of his seat and asked him, 'Does your eye hurt?' Hans moved his eyes left and right and replied that when he moved his eyeball, something was bothering him. Perhaps it was scratched. Helmut ran out of the casemate. Hans was given an eye patch and his bundle to carry under his arm. 'Hold on and take care of yourself!' He shook hands and marched off. Everything in those days was chaotic. All the casemates were full of wounded soldiers, as well as the rally point and the nearest doctor around the corner. Hans was lost to me. When I visited West Germany for the first time in 1949, Austria was no longer part of Greater Germany. I had other problems over the years, and when foreign travel started I found that Austria is a big country if you are just looking for one man.

We were assigned a new Obergefreiter from the 500th Assault Gun Training and Reserve Battalion (Sturmgeschütz Ersatz und Ausbildung Abtailung 500). He was a calm man, but during the last few days we had left, we did not really manage to make friends with him.

Infantry soldiers intercepted a supply container that had been parachuted in because there was no way Ju-52s could land. We had little ammunition, so shells for the 105-mm howitzers were also dropped in these containers. Some of the pods landed with the Russians, so they knew excatly what we were missing. We drove around for twenty-four hours and when I got in I knew something was not quite right. The next morning, I looked closely and saw that the howitzer's gun had been removed and a 20-mm anti-aircraft gun had been fitted instead and secured with some wire. However, we still had 20-mm ammunition, and with the contents of the crates laid out in front of me on the ground, I examined everything carefully. At one point I said, 'Helmut, if "Ivan" really attacks today, we'll have to stop him quickly. But not with this. They'll just fall over laughing!'

We joked, and I added that the Allied bomber pilots, flying at low altitude, had a lot of respect for automatic 20-mm anti-aircraft guns that fired four barrels simultaneously. Here, on the other hand, we inserted each shell separately and fired a single shot each time.

Above and below: Two photographs showing a destroyed StuG Ausf. G in the Citadel, near the North Gate. The corpses of German soldiers can clearly be seen nearby.

There was no room for a loader in the vehicle. The new gunner was silent, and the tone between loader and commander was new to him. Helmut was very well-mannered and did not show his annoyance. We never fired a single shot that day. The Russians were also silent.

The next day there was another exchange, and we were once again in our old sector, where we had started our fight in Poznań. The gun still had ammunition, but it was probably all that was left. One thing had changed: the spare chest was empty. Nothing was wasted, and we knew that nothing could fall into the wrong hands when the end came. The end was unpredictable. The only certainty was that before it happened, we would try to get out.

The evening of 22 February came, and the moment that we had all imagined would happen differently. Late in the evening, at the corner where the Szelag cemetery turns into an empty field, we received an order: 'Destroy the guns!' It was a great shock and for the first time, I had the impression that everything was falling apart. Our guns, these weapons that had never let us down, we were supposed to destroy ourselves. The key here was that the enemy was not to hear any explosions. I had been a soldier for a year and a half before I was taken prisoner, and this final order was one I obeyed very reluctantly. But it was done. We dismantled the locks, destroyed the viewfinders. Sepp sabotaged the engine by taking out the spark plugs and putting sand, grease and snow in the cylinder. We ran the battery down, ripped out the cables, and after half an hour it was all over. The gun was useless. No one would even bother trying to use it.

We met at the North Gate, where we sat in the dark, watching others push ahead. There were whispers, and suddenly one of our comrades, who had already survived Russian captivity in 1914-18, said: 'If we're taken prisoners ... many of us will die ... many died then ... epidemics ... Russian food ... .wet... soggy bread... cabbage soup... there was nothing for our stomachs... raw porridge... thick millet or barley ... many of us got sick.' (That was the first time I heard the word kasha).

Suddenly, we heard the Hauptmann's firm voice: 'Who wants to try to escape on their own? I'm not giving orders anymore. Who wants to take the risk?'

There were 100-150 people lined up, and we all headed in the same direction we had just come from about half an hour earlier. We missed the Tiger; there was a well on the left which Siegert had said they often lay flat next to because the handle made so much noise. We crouched down to hide as shell fragments flew over our heads. Later, the road led through an open field. Just at that moment, the rhythmic tak-tak-tak of the Russian machine gun started near the cemetery. We scattered and threw ourselves on the ground. Our group moved forward and the Russians fell silent. No one fired anymore. We were no match for the MG-42's shearing fire, but we were not easy targets in that darkness either.

A Tiger next to the house where its crew was quartered. Its gunner was Richard Siegert, later the author of the memoir *The Tiger from Poznań*.

Without defending ourselves in any way, we simply ran away. There was no line of defence. Our commander noticed that the area between the Zeppelinwiese and the bank of the River Warta was only occupied sporadically. The next break through in this area was completely different; the men ran straight into the fire. We fled north at night, through marshy meadows, paths, gardens and orchards, always following the leader of the group. Someone mentioned the village of Oborniki and the forest nearby and that there were closed forest areas between the Warta and Noteć rivers.

The group was a bit chaotic, and every now and then someone was right on the commander's heels. Sometimes someone slipped. Finally, a shot was fired from behind. We did not know if it was some idiot who had failed to secure his gun, or someone from the opposite side pretending to be one of us and infiltrating the enemy ranks.

As soon as it got light, the forest began. We made our way through, and on the other side were fields stretching for 1.5-2 kilometres. Perhaps it would have been better to make our way in small groups in the semi-darkness? Who knows?

Suddenly, someone decided that we should stop and hide during the day. But where and how? Someone started eating. A colleague in front of me was dipping herring in tomato sauce. Finally, he handed me half a can: 'Eat, Alfred, I've had enough.' Just fifteen minutes later, the man was dead. Shot in the head when we encountered the Russians. Years later, his sister would ask me about the circumstances of his death.

There were suddenly gunshots and noises behind us. The Polish militia were combing the forest, so we ran away. The unit was focused on escaping, not on combat. We ran to the right, but should we have to run to the left? All at once, an opening appeared in front of us. We were stood on the edge of a slightly wooded area and, 40-45 metres in front of us, were thirty or forty half-hidden Russians with submachine guns. They waved, laughed, and shouted at us, wanting to take us prisoner. We started to run, and soon the first one of us fell.

Before I could collect myself, a Russian appeared in front of me. My friend Leopold (from Hetzer's crew) said that they must have already crossed the mountain of hay in the field. It was an ambush; they must have been watching us for a long time.

What happened to us next has been told many times before. We stood for the initial search, watches first, then weapons. Three T-34 tanks stood off to the side. I took off my cap for a second and felt a moment of freedom and joy that the war was over, and I had survived. I had no idea what was waiting for us, or how many of us would survive it. I was convinced nothing would happen to me, and was almost curious about the Russians, whom I watched with interest. They stood apart, laughing and smoking cigarettes. Then I thought to myself: 'I feel sorry for you. There's still fighting going on on the River Oder. You don't know if you'll survive.' Not everyone thinks like that, but it was how I felt at the time. The battle for Poznań was over. My captivity had begun.

German veterans from the Sturmgeschütz Brigade "Grossdeutschland" next to a plaque dedicated to their comrades who died in Poznań. Second from left is Diddo Diddens.

Alfred Kriehn and Maciej Karalus, a historian specialising in the fight for Poznań, during the last meeting of German veterans at Oberfeldwebel Josef Schreiber barracks in Immendingen, Germany, in 2007.

Notes

1. These ditches were actually dug in the summer of 1944, mainly by Polish civilians, on the orders of the German occupiers.
2. Obergefreiter Johannes Ströcker was previously one of the soldiers of the 1st Battery of the Sturmgeschütz Brigade "Grossdeutschland", commanded by the ace of German assault artillery, Oberleutnant Diddo Diddens. Among its many actions, it participated in the destruction of heavy anti-tank guns and three tanks on 25 April 1944 near the town of Jessy, Russia. For this action, Oberleutnant Diddens was awarded the Knight's Cross.
3. The transport was commanded by Oberwachtmeister Anton Reif, previously a platoon commander in the 1st Battery of the Sturmgeschütz Brigade "Grossdeutschland". He was awarded the Iron Cross 2nd Class on 5 July 1941, the Iron Cross 1st Class on 29 July 1942, and the German Cross in Gold on 27 July 1944.
4. The 8th Sturmgeschütz Division "Grossdeutschland" consisted of sixteen soldiers who had previously accompanied the transport: A. Kriehn and two of his retreating companions from Kutno, Oberleutnant Halmann and his driver, one infantry soldier who had previously served in the assault artillery, and ten soldiers of the 500th School Auxiliary Battalion of Assault Guns. A total of thirty-two men, four for each of the eight guns.
5. The term Sturmgeschütz (commonly StuG) includes assault guns armed with a 75-mm cannon, such as: Sturmgeschütz III with 75-mm assault gun 40L/24 (SdKfz 142), Sturmgeschütz III with

75-mm assault gun 40L/48 (SdKfz 142/1), Sturmgeschütz IV with 75-mm assault gun 40L/48 (SdKfz 167). A Sturmgeschütz armed with a 105-mm howitzer was referred to as a Sturmhaubitze or StuH. Its full name was: Sturmgeschütz III 105-mm Sturmhaubitze 42L/28 (SdKfz 142/2).

6. Zeppelinwiese, the so-called "Zeppelin's Meadow" had an airship landing pad and, during the Battle of Poznań, acted as a German airfield in the northern part of the city.

7. The Junkers Ju-52 was often colloquially referred to by German soldiers as "Tante Ju", meaning "Aunt Ju".

8. A Katyusha rocket launcher.

9. In reality, the new name was the Park-Monument of the Brotherhood in Arms and Polish-Soviet Friendship. In 1992, the name was changed to Citadel Park.

HISTORY BROUGHT BACK TO LIFE WITH PEN & SWORD BOOKS

Pen & Sword Books have over 6000 books currently available and we cover all periods of history on land, sea and air.

If you would like to hear more about our other titles sign up now and receive 30% off your next purchase. www.penandswordbooks.com/newsletter/

By signing up to our free discounts, reviews on new releases, previews of forthcoming titles and upcoming competitions, so you will never miss out!

Not online? Return this card to us with your contact details and we will put you on our catalog mailing list.

Mr/Mrs/Ms ....

Address..

Zip Code.................... Email address...

Website: www.penandswordbooks.com
Email: Uspen-and-sword@casematepublishers.com · Telephone: (610) 853-9131
Stay in touch: facebook.com/penandswordbooks or follow us on Twitter @penswordbooks

We hope you enjoyed this book!

Pen and Sword Books
c/o Casemate Publishers
1950 Lawrence Road
Havertown, PA 19083